PARENTING

CLUES FOR THE CLUELESS

CHRISTOPHER D. HUDSON

KATIE E. GIESER

CAROL R. FIELDING

MARYANN LACKLAND

CAROL SMITH

RANDY SOUTHERN

LEN WOODS

PROMISE
PRESS
An Imprint of Barbour Publishing

Parenting Clues for the Clueless
© 1999 by Barbour Publishing, Inc. All rights reserved.

Developed and produced by the Livingstone Corporation.

Interior Design by Design Corps, Batavia, IL.

Cover Design by Robyn Martins.

Cover and Interior Artwork by Elwood Smith.

ISBN: 1-57748-673-0

Published by: Promise Press, an imprint of Barbour Publishing, Inc., P.O. Box 719
               Uhrichsville, OH 44683.

Printed in the United States of America.

TABLE OF CONTENTS

SECTION 1
A GLEAM IN YOUR EYE 1

SECTION 2
WHO RUNS THE HOUSE? 25

SECTION 3
WHAT EVERY FAMILY NEEDS 37

SECTION 4
NURTURE 59

SECTION 5
SPIRITUAL DEVELOPMENT 87

SECTION 6
DISCIPLINE 99

SECTION 7
INFANTS 119

SECTION 11
HIGH SCHOOLER 195

SECTION 12
RECOVERING FROM THE WORST 221

INDEX   235

....

INTRODUCTION

Your precious little bundle of joy is screaming at the top of her teeny little lungs, and all you can think is. . .I've got eighteen more years of this?!

You overhear your middle schooler using colorful language that she didn't learn from you. You gasp and wonder, Where did my sweet little girl learn to talk like that?

Your teenage son wants to borrow the car to attend a party. . .You hand over the keys, but you're really wondering, Should I even be letting him go?

Break out your questions and lay aside your worries! The folks at *Clues for the Clueless* have done it again by bringing an award-winning (at least in *our* hearts) book to tackle yet another of life's curve balls, in this case, parenting.

So you aren't exactly June Cleaver, and your family may never be mistaken for the Huxtables. But you're a parent, in the midst of the challenging, rewarding, and often overwhelming process of raising your kids.

This book will help you sort through the mazes of discipline, finicky eaters, and curfews; as well as help you relate to your offspring who look to you for a hand to cross the street. . .or the keys to the car. Read about these topics and everything in between. . .even tips on keeping your sanity! More specifically you'll find:

CATCH A CLUE

A Truckload of Clues. You'll learn tips from parents who survived parenting. . .and enjoyed it!

WIDE ANGLE

Perspective. It's easy to get caught up in the day-to-day tasks of picking up stray socks, packing another lunch, and driving to pom-pom practice. But parenting is so much more than that, and sometimes we need help looking at the big picture. We'll help you take a step back.

WOW!

Humorous Stories. At the time, you may feel like bursting into tears, but those moments often turn out to be the funniest stories later. We've collected a few choice ones for you.

DON'T FORGET

Important Reminders. Certain things are important to remember as you're in the midst of parenting. We've highlighted those for you.

THE BOTTOM LINE

The Bottom Line. We'll help you get beyond confusion by letting you know the most important stuff to remember.

THE BIBLE SAYS

Help from Above. We've highlighted a few key Bible verses that will encourage you in your day-to-day parenting challenges.

Before you drown your parenting woes in a lukewarm glass of cherry Kool-Aid, you've got to do one thing: *Read this book!* Feel free to read it *your* way: from cover to cover or skipping around to the parts that interest you most. No matter how you read it, you'll find it's jammed with good advice, great ideas, and entertaining thoughts. So turn the page and start reading. . . . You'll be glad you did!

SECTION 1

A GLEAM IN YOUR EYE

WHAT WILL IT BE LIKE TO GROW UP IN THE 21ST CENTURY?

Parent to child in 1690s—"Fill thine cornucopia with corn husks before sunrise, young Winthrop, or thou shalt be scourged with the rod!"

Parent to child in 1790s—"In the course of human events, Thomas, it has become necessary for you to do your ciphering."

Parent to child in 1890s—"Help circle the wagons, Willie! And stay low!"

Parent to child in 1990s—"Turn off the VCR and get in the van, Dylan! We'll just have to go through the drive thru on the way to soccer practice!"

Parent to child in 2090s—"Your transporter pod has been activated, R-3/D-3. Prepare for a linkup at Shimdar 81S at 1600."

What *will* life be like for kids growing up in the twenty-first century?

Who can say, really? Trend-watchers and futurists have all sorts of predictions, but that's all they are: guesstimations.

At your Clues for the Clueless International Research Center, we've done our own studies and polls. We've concluded that, if Christ doesn't come back, the only things we can know for sure about the immediate future are that:

1. Technological advancements will continue to leap forward at stunning rates.
2. Dick Clark will continue to look about thirty years old.
3. Based on current trends, the average professional athlete will earn (single-handedly and annually) more than the gross national product of South America, but it won't really matter because. . .
4. Bill Gates will have enough money to purchase everything north of the equator.
5. Millions of moronic people will still keep spending hundreds of millions of dollars on psychics (who are laughing all the way to the proverbial bank).

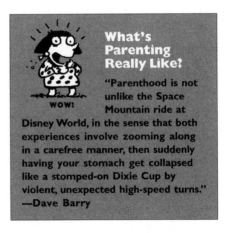

What's Parenting Really Like?

WOW!

"Parenthood is not unlike the Space Mountain ride at Disney World, in the sense that both experiences involve zooming along in a carefree manner, then suddenly having your stomach get collapsed like a stomped-on Dixie Cup by violent, unexpected high-speed turns."
—Dave Barry

Ah, the future. It *is* kind of exciting. . .and scary! The great unknown. Imagine our forefathers at the dawn of the twentieth century. There's no way they possibly could have imagined the cataclysmic changes just ahead. Two terrible world wars! Manned flight! SPACE voyages to the moon

and beyond! The eradication of
deadly diseases! The discovery of
new plagues! What about television? Computers?! The Internet?!!
Even simple things like air
conditioning? Flushing toilets?
Cars? Traffic jams?!! People *in* cars,
stuck *in* massive traffic jams,
talking via cellular phones to
colleagues around the world!?!?!?
Elvis? Rap music?

Children Are...

THE BIBLE SAYS

"Sons are a heritage from the LORD, children a reward from him. Like arrows in the hands of a warrior are sons born in one's youth. Blessed is the man whose quiver is full of them." (Psalm 127:3–5)

Yes, the future will feature lots
of surprises and mysteries. But when it comes to the question of children,
we shouldn't let fear of the unknown determine whether we become
parents. Consider two of the more common "future concerns" that many
couples cite as reasons to not "bring kids* into this world."

"The world is gross and getting worse all the time!"

No doubt about it. The lines between good and evil are becoming ever
clearer. There's an "in-your-face!" perversity in this generation that is both
shocking and disturbing. But it's not as though this trend represents a real
change in the human race.

Remember Attila the Hun? The Vikings? Go back even further. Read
Genesis 6. Study the Book of Judges. Ever since the Fall in Eden, the
human race has been utterly depraved and twisted. Through the ages,
social conventions and/or spiritual revivals have occasionally put the
brakes on crassness. But in other eras, decadence has flourished. This
moral ebb and flow has always existed and it always will until Christ
comes back and makes all things right.

The point? Society may decay even more, **or** we may be on the verge of

*Obviously here (and throughout the book) we'll be using the terms "kid" and "kids" to
refer to precious human offspring and not young goats.

a sovereign movement of the Spirit of God which could result in a cultural about-face. Who knows?

Someone has suggested that if Christian couples living now decided to rear a generation of kids to love and serve the Lord wholeheartedly, that alone might turn the tide.

"Child-rearing is getting so expensive; only the rich can afford to have kids!"

Excellent insight, grasshopper! You're two for two. You've obviously priced disposable diapers and the cost of orthodontia in recent weeks. No question, having children is a major expense (we'll talk more about that in upcoming chapters).

And yet, lots of low-income people manage to do it and many

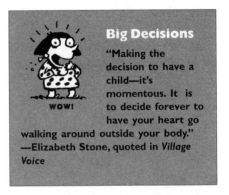

Big Decisions

"Making the decision to have a child—it's momentous. It is to decide forever to have your heart go walking around outside your body."
—Elizabeth Stone, quoted in *Village Voice*

WOW!

of them do it quite well. Meaning we ought to rethink much of what our culture says about the costs of child rearing. If we yield to Madison Avenue's slick pressure to provide our children with the best and most of everything, it's definitely pricey, but there are alternatives, as we will see.

WHAT'S THE BOTTOM LINE?

According to the Bible, children are **not** a pain, a burden, a bother, an inconvenience, or a liability. No, they're a reward and a blessing. They're gifts from God! (See Psalm 127)

And if we rear them to know and love and serve the Lord, and then if we shoot them like arrows out into all corners of our culture, maybe, just maybe, we can turn this thing around. At the very least, we can be faithful to have an impact on our generation, which is all God asks of us.

Will it be scary? Absolutely. To walk your precious offspring into a classroom taught by a complete stranger is unnerving. To see your sweet child step onto a basketball court with bigger, tougher kids is enough to make you want to throw up.

But as believers in Jesus, we have certain bedrock promises we can rely upon. Our kids (or would-be kids) will be held securely by a God Who is utterly faithful, completely good, and perfectly wise. Besides all this, He has all power. Our times—and our kids' times—are in His hand.

You *can* trust the Lord in the great adventure of parenting, no matter what lies ahead in the twenty-first century!

START WITH A STRONG MARRIAGE

There's an old saying that "you can't make a good omelet with bad eggs."

Now, if this were a *cookbook*, that would be a helpful bit of advice. Unfortunately this is a book on **_parenting_**. So perhaps we need to adjust that metaphor a bit:

"If you're trying to whip up an appealing family in the great banquet of life, you need to begin with essential quality ingredients in the expensive skillet of marriage."

Still unclear? Okay, how about:

"Healthy homes begin with strong marriages."

No matter how you say it or what metaphors you employ, the point is a strong marriage is foundational to the rearing of healthy children.

Clearly we live in an era when marriage is viewed with disdain. Look at the talk shows, the magazines, the portrayals of marriage in the media. Depending on the program or article or

No Experience Required

"Making a baby is one of the greatest nonskilled acts in the world. It requires virtually no experience, no talent, and no expertise. People who can't type, use chopsticks, throw a Frisbee straight, work a VCR, or hold down a job can make a baby."
—**Erma Bombeck**

WOW!

pontificating celebrity, marriage is deemed "unnecessary." "Unpleasant." "Optional." "Old-fashioned." "Confining."

Perhaps this explains why millions of couples are cohabitating and more and more children are being born out of wedlock. A few years ago when Vice President Dan Quayle publicly criticized the writers and producers of the popular television show *Murphy Brown* for a plot line involving its main character having a child out of wedlock, he was castigated as a prude and worse. But over the next couple of years, the research began confirming Quayle's concerns. Eventually an *Atlantic Monthly* cover story proclaimed, "Dan Quayle Was Right," and reported the empirical findings that kids simply do better in homes where there's both a loving mom and dad.

This shouldn't surprise us. The first institution in the Bible is *marriage* (Genesis 2:18–25)—not the *family*, per se. When you piece together the first two chapters of the Bible and realize that chapter 2 is really just an in-depth account of 1:26–28, you realize it was only after the first wedding—performed by God Himself—that the new bride and groom (Eve and Adam, respectively) were commissioned to be fruitful and multiply and fill the earth.

Does this mean that any man and woman with a valid marriage license can provide a healthy home life for children? Unfortunately, no. You don't have to be Dan Quayle to realize that not every marriage is a healthy environment for kids.

Don't Believe It!

CATCH A CLUE

There's a common myth that one way a couple in marital trouble can overcome their relational difficulties is to have a baby together. This is like two mountain climbers on a weak, crumbling ledge deciding to save themselves by bringing another climber (and more weight!) onto their disintegrating perch.

A baby *won't* make a bad marriage better. It will add tension. If you're already having trouble getting along, what do you think is going to happen when you add sleeplessness, extra financial pressures, and a host of new responsibilities to the mix?

So how does a couple know if their marriage is strong enough to sustain kids? Below are seven indicators of a strong marriage. This is not an exhaustive list, but a couple with these qualities would be head and shoulders above the pack.

QUALITIES OF A STRONG MARRIAGE

- ## *Maturity*
  Children don't need to be having children. Or as Eda LeShan, the family counselor and author, once put it: "If you are a parent, it helps if you are a grown-up."

  Realize you can be forty and immature; or you can be twenty-three and ready for the task of parenting. Mature couples take life's irritations and problems in stride, a quality much required in dealing with babies, whom someone once described as "elongated intestinal tracts with loud noises at one end and no responsibility at the other."

- ## *A shared, strong, abiding faith*
  Couples who are growing closer to Christ inevitably grow closer together. This gives them a solid spiritual foundation on which to build a healthy home. Why? They have access to supernatural resources of love, patience, gentleness, etc.

- ## *Commitment*
  The couple who says: "We're in this thing (i.e., marriage) for the long haul. We meant it when we promised "till death do us part". . .*that's* the couple that offers promise and hope and a future to a newborn. If kids

were given the choice, do you think they'd elect to become part of a family that is threatening to disintegrate?

- **Unselfishness**

Good relationships aren't 50-50 propositions. They're 100-100 arrangements, where each spouse gives all he/she has, all the time. There's no scorekeeping, only an active desire to put the other first (his/her interests, needs, desires, etc. over one's own).

If this quality is lacking in your relationship, realize a trip to the maternity ward isn't going to magically produce it.

- **Communication**

Healthy couples talk about everything. They listen to one another, and they follow biblical guidelines in resolving conflict. Couples without these habits are inviting trouble when they decide to bring a new life into the home equation. A child becomes one more thing *not* to communicate about—and hence, one more thing to fight about!

- **Respect**

When you know your spouse isn't perfect, but you still admire him or her, you've got respect. When you'd consider your kid lucky to have a mom/ dad like your partner, you've got what it takes.

- **Humor**

Can you laugh together? At yourselves? If not, what are you going to do when that undiapered newborn "projectile poops" into your lap? When that toddler puts his popsicle in the VCR?

The couples who don't take life too seriously make the best marriage partners and the healthiest parents.

If you want to know more about having a healthy marriage (and who doesn't?) consult the excellent, funny, informative *Marriage Clues for the Clueless.*

ARE YOU READY?

Hah, hah, hah, hah, hah.
Good one.
"Are you ready?" Hah, hah, hah, hah.

Well now, seriously, we probably *shouldn't* joke about such an earnest question. Here you are trying to answer one of the great questions of life. You're contemplating one of the most serious personal issues a married couple can ponder, and we're over here laughing it off. You bought this book because you wanted *help*, not mocking sarcasm. So here goes:

SIGNS YOU'RE *NOT* READY FOR PARENTHOOD:

You're not married and have no plans to tie the knot.

Your spouse's biggest concern just now is passing the eleventh grade.

You baby-sat a friend's sleeping infant last month for thirty minutes and felt really "trapped."

In your mind, you've narrowed it down to either: (a) a new baby or (b) redoing the kitchen.

You like being able to schedule everything in your Day•Timer® and it infuriates you when anything or anyone (even your spouse) disrupts your plans.

Mulder & Sculley keep stopping by to ask you questions because they think you may be carrying an alien life force.

You see yourself as the center of the universe, and you really like the view from there.

Actually there's serious question whether anyone is ever truly "ready" for parenthood. It's one of those things you can read about, analyze, and listen to others talk about, but, rather like trying to get a kitten out of a tree, you can't fully appreciate the experience till you're in the middle of it.

Amateurs

"Parenthood remains the greatest single preserve of the amateur."
— Alvin Toffler

WOW!

It's important to remember that for every "negative" aspect in the parenting process, there's one (or MORE!) "positive." Consider:

You think you're *not* ready for. . .	But could you be ready for. . .
Gaining twenty to forty pounds!	The wondrous kicking of a life—a life YOU helped create—inside you!?
The agony of labor!	The joy of holding that precious newborn in your arms?
A screaming baby with colic!	A cooing infant who smiles when he sees you or even hears your voice?
Paying big doctor bills!	Bonding with your own child by rocking her to sleep?
Sleepless nights!	Miraculous moments too mysterious and marvelous to put into words?

An abrupt change in your sex life!	The exquisite pleasure of feeling soft little hands pat your face? Or the exhilaration of your child's first slobbery kiss?
Loads of baby paraphernalia!	The fact that much of this will be given or loaned to you by loving family, friends, and neighbors?
Fewer opportunities to get out and socialize!	Total strangers remarking about how gorgeous and cute your child is?
Poopy diapers!	The sheer elation you and your spouse will feel when your kid completes toilet training?
Toddlers messing with your "stuff"!	Toddlers giving you more delight in one day than all your "stuff" can give you in a lifetime?
Having the heavy responsibility of rearing a child in such a gross world!	The joy of rearing sweet kids who have a desire to rock the world for Christ?

The fact is, parenthood, despite all the horror stories you hear, is a blessed experience. Charles Osgood of CBS News may have said it best, "Babies are always more trouble than you thought—and more wonderful."

So maybe we should rephrase the question at the beginning of the

Priorities

"A hundred years from now . . .it will not matter what my bank account was, the sort of house I lived in, or the kind of car I drove. . .but the world may be different because I was important in the life of a child."
—**Source unknown**

WIDE ANGLE

chapter. Perhaps we should ask, Are you ready for a one-of-a-kind life experience that can:

- ### *Force you to grow?*

  Peter De Vries once quipped, "The value of marriage is not that adults produce children, but that children produce adults."

  Realize as a parent you'll be stretched and pulled and challenged like never before. And if you and your spouse handle it with love and trust, God will use the experience to conform both of you to the image of Christ (Romans 8:28–29).

- ### *Teach you to sacrifice?*

  A comment by Jean Kerr says it all: "The thing about having a baby is that thereafter you have it." In other words, parenting is not intended to be just a moonlighting venture; it's a lifelong, full-time commitment.

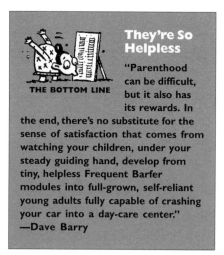

THE BOTTOM LINE

They're So Helpless

"Parenthood can be difficult, but it also has its rewards. In the end, there's no substitute for the sense of satisfaction that comes from watching your children, under your steady guiding hand, develop from tiny, helpless Frequent Barfer modules into full-grown, self-reliant young adults fully capable of crashing your car into a day-care center."
—**Dave Barry**

One Atlanta man, Walter, put it this way:

> "The main lesson my wife and I learned with our first child was just how selfish we were. Suddenly we had this infant who didn't understand our needs or desires. If he was hungry and crying, we couldn't just say, 'Hey, could you wait till this TV show is over or until we finish our conversation?' The whole 'baby' experience taught me how obsessed

I was with *me* and *my* agenda. And how much I resented anyone messing with *my* life or *my* marital relationship. I suppose I knew in my head that the Christian life is all about dying to self and living for God and others. But this was a situation where I had to make a choice: Either live that truth out or be a selfish pig and a parental disgrace."

- ### *Give you deeper insight into love?*
  Never mind the fact that most newborns look like Mr. Magoo after he's been pulled through a port-hole—you'll think your kid is the most beautiful creature on Earth. As a new parent, you will fall crazy in head-over-heels love with this sweet little bundle. You'll show strangers his pictures, you'll talk publicly and proudly about her bowel movements, yes, even their number and color.

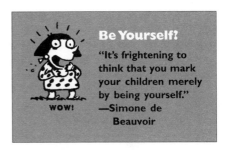

Be Yourself?

"It's frightening to think that you mark your children merely by being yourself."
—Simone de Beauvoir

WOW!

For a long time the relationship will be almost completely one-sided. As your child grows, you'll have a better sense of how God feels when His children are hurting or straying. As one who sacrifices much for his/her child, you'll get a taste of ingratitude and being taken for granted. Over the years you'll have excellent (and numerous!) opportunities to practice unconditional love and forgiveness.

You were thinking maybe you had the "love thing" down? Hah—have a kid or two and then come back and see us.

WHEN SHOULD YOU HAVE CHILDREN?

The award-winning, scientifically astute *Clues for the Clueless* research team knows of certain married couples who are so explosively fertile they have to exercise extreme caution (even making eye contact or holding hands could be dangerous) while in the presence of one another. For such couples, a French *laissez-faire* attitude toward intimacy could easily result in, oh, eighteen to twenty children in a fifteen-to twenty-year-span of marriage.

One young couple in Louisiana, with four children, scheduled each of their conception and delivery dates in the wife's appointment book so as to coincide (and not interfere) with important family events.

Another young Texas couple with five children under the age of seven, might be willing to state (if they weren't theologically conservative, orthodox Christians) that their most recent child was born without the benefit of sexual intimacy. We're talking one *very* fertile couple!

On the other hand, there are many other couples who have the opposite problem. Conception is a difficult proposition, and the "if" question is beginning to overshadow the question of "when."

Either way, all this raises the issue of timing. When should couples strive to have children? We'll explore the issue of "family planning" in the next chapter. But for now, consider the. . .

Best times to have a child:

A "random, nationwide poll of married couples"* reveals the following gold mine of information about the optimal time for giving birth:

---

*Conducted by "scientifically" remembered comments made by friends
around the country about the whole birthing process

- Preferably nine months (at least) after you say "I do"
- Once you actually get inside the hospital (and not in the car or the cab on the way)
- When your deductible is completely paid
- In the spring (before the hot summer months)
- Midmorning (not too early, not too late in the day)
- After a very fast, very mild labor
- When your husband is home (and not away on business or hunting, fishing, playing golf, etc.)
- Anytime *after* you get your epidural (NOT before!)
- Not during Oprah or Rosie O'Donnell
- Whenever the sweetest mother-in-law can be there to cook, clean, and help
- When your friends who are your same size are NOT pregnant (so that you can borrow all their maternity clothes)

Worst times to have a child:

- When your big, overriding concern is that your biological clock is ticking down
- When your reasoning is, "I've got a condo, a mountain bike, a food processor, a home gym. Now, I think I'd like to see what it's like to have a kid."
- When your motive is "I want somebody to need me."
- When your motive is "I want someone I can control."
- When your motive is "I want to live life over again vicariously through another."
- When your marriage is rocky and you find yourself thinking, "A baby would help bring us closer."

- When you catch yourself thinking, "Maybe if I give her a kid, she'll shut up and leave me alone."

SIX INDICATORS THAT IT MIGHT BE TIME FOR KIDS...

1. **When you're willing to pour yourself out for another**
   Consider the commitment of a Laysan albatross tracked in 1998 by biologists from Wake Forest. This devoted mother traveled more than 24,800 miles in only ninety days in its unrelenting quest to find food for its chick. What a model of sacrifice!

2. **When you're ready to be stretched (literally, ladies!) and challenged**
   Heh, heh, a little "stretch mark" humor there. Heh, heh.

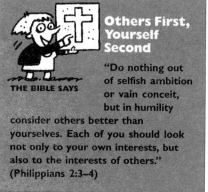

Others First, Yourself Second

THE BIBLE SAYS

"Do nothing out of selfish ambition or vain conceit, but in humility consider others better than yourselves. Each of you should look not only to your own interests, but also to the interests of others." (Philippians 2:3–4)

3. **When you're okay with "not being in control" of much of anything anymore**

4. **When you're comfortable with radically changing your priorities and your routine**

5. **When you're committed to being a parent who takes seriously the stewardship of rearing children to the glory of God**

6. **When you are serious about being a role model for the next generation**

You will not have the freedom you once had. As a parent, you will have a whole new slew of responsibilities and commitments. So now is the time to decide if you are willing to give your time, your energy, your resources, your self, your LIFE away for the benefit of another. (Actually, you should already be doing this with your

It Conflicts

"We need to realize that . . . we can't have everything. Career and money issues are in direct conflict with parenting responsibilities."
—Robert Vernon

spouse, and now all this "baby talk" is a discussion about adding another—little—person to the mix.)

If you're in a place where you're trying to figure out the best time to start a family (and you probably are or you wouldn't be reading this chapter), it's important to remember that God is sovereign over the universe and over our lives. God's *sovereignty* means that He's in complete control and nothing happens that He doesn't either cause or allow. Coupled with His goodness and grace, this means that those who love and trust God can rest in the comfortable truth that He will send children (if we are to have children) at the very best time.

His schedule may not jibe with ours, but His timing is always perfect (because He is perfectly wise). There are no accidental pregnancies. From heaven's perspective, there are no deliveries that come too late or too early. God's timing is never suspect or "off."

IS FAMILY PLANNING BAD?

The notion of "family planning" (i.e., couples deciding how many children they intend to have and when) is controversial in many quarters.

Some believe that God gave sex solely for the purpose of *procreation* (i.e., having children). Therefore birth control devices essentially reduce the marriage act to a matter of *recreation*, which cheapens intercourse and robs it of its awesome mystery.

Others think the whole idea smacks of "playing God." Isn't it arrogant, they argue, to presume upon the will of a good and wise God about what is best for our lives or our potential children's

Will Life Change?

Will children change your life?

THE BOTTOM LINE

Absolutely. Totally. Irrevocably.

lives, or for the world? To rely on human ideas and resort to man-made means to prevent conception is to usurp the role and the prerogatives of the Creator. Also, they might insist, the very act of trying to limit the number of one's offspring is at odds with the scriptural declaration that children are a blessing from God.

Many sincere believers feel strongly that the acceptance of any form of birth control puts one on the slippery slope that ultimately leads to abortion: "If we say it's okay to play God *before* conception, how can we argue that it's illegitimate *afterward?*" Also, the fact that many so-called "pro-choice" groups are such staunch advocates of "family planning" makes the practice highly suspect in the eyes of many Christians.

On the other side of the coin are those who believe that God gave sex for *procreation*, yes, but also for *celebration*—as a physical way to express the spiritual and emotional oneness between a committed husband and wife. These believers would further argue that God expects us to exercise good judgment in the affairs of everyday life. Most folks prayerfully and carefully plan for all sorts of things in life: an education, a career, an annual budget, career changes, retirement, etc. For this they receive commendation. At the same time most people (even Christians) look with contempt at the shortsighted individual who gets in trouble because he fails to think ahead. The person who foolishly doesn't consider the long-term consequences of his/her actions is looked upon with condemnation!

So which is it: One group says family planning is bad; another group says it's wise. Who's right? Who's wrong? Maybe we'd be wise to see what the Bible says about planning in general. Consider the following verses:

"Plans fail for lack of counsel, but with many advisers they succeed" (Proverbs 15:22).

The point? **Planning (if based on wise counsel) can lead to success.**

"The plans of the diligent lead to profit as surely as haste leads to poverty" (Proverbs 21:5).

The point? **Not only is planning profitable, but impulsiveness can be disastrous!**

"Trust in the LORD with all your heart and lean not on your own understanding; in all your ways acknowledge him, and he will make your paths straight" (Proverbs 3:5–6).

The point? **Any planning we do must be rooted in deep faith and based on God's higher wisdom, not on mere worldly notions.**

"Therefore do not worry about tomorrow, for tomorrow will worry about itself. Each day has enough trouble of its own" (Matthew 6:34).

The point? **Planning for the future might be okay, but worrying about the future never is.**

"Many are the plans in a man's heart, but it is the Lord's purpose that prevails" (Proverbs 19:21).

The point? **God is sovereign and can override our "wise plans" no matter what we do.**

It comes down to this: The world is full of couples who have said, "We're going to wait four years and *then* start our family!" Imagine their surprise when eight or ten or twelve years later their nursery is still empty.

The world is also full of couples who have said, "We're going to wait four years and *then* start a family!"—only for the wife to get pregnant on their honeymoon, despite using a supposed "highly reliable" form of birth control!

As in most situations of life, there is a balance to be struck here. We should be wise. We should be prayerful. We should use sanctified common sense. Most of all, we should submit to the greater purposes of God. Hey, He has the ultimate "veto" or "trump" power anyway!

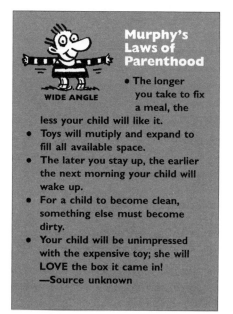

WIDE ANGLE

Murphy's Laws of Parenthood

- The longer you take to fix a meal, the less your child will like it.
- Toys will mutiply and expand to fill all available space.
- The later you stay up, the earlier the next morning your child will wake up.
- For a child to become clean, something else must become dirty.
- Your child will be unimpressed with the expensive toy; she will LOVE the box it came in!
—**Source unknown**

REASONS TO PRAYERFULLY DELAY GETTING PREGNANT

1. You are at an unsettled place in your marriage (i.e., your relationship with your spouse isn't exactly healthy and strong).
2. You are facing severe financial problems that are creating severe stress in your marriage.
3. One or both of you is, frankly, immature (spiritually, emotionally, relationally).
4. One or both parties has no desire to alter his/her/their current lifestyle.
5. You have questions about a preexisting medical condition that might endanger your life or the life of your baby.

SECTION 2
WHO RUNS THE HOUSE?

THE COST OF SACRIFICE

The temptation in a book like this is to trumpet all the glories of parenting and to soft-sell the hard realities. As already discussed, parenting **is** a wonderful experience; however, it also requires tremendous sacrifice (if you're going to do it in a way that pleases God). Here's just a partial list:

Putting others first—a bawling, hungry infant doesn't care that you'd rather finish your video than administer another feeding.

Financial hit—from pregnancy to babyhood and all the way through college, children require monetary support (which explains why so many parents take extra jobs).

WOW!

Is All the Sacrifice Worth It?

Consider the following story told by Olympic chronicler, Bud Greenspan:

"Bill Hanover. . .in 1924 was the best rower in the country and was about to go to Paris to win a gold medal—he couldn't lose. But just before the Olympics team was getting ready to leave, his wife went into labor. The doctors, his wife, his friends all urged him to go. He stayed for the birth of his son.

"He was never really sure he made the right decision until many years later during the summer of 1952. That's when he got a telegram from Helsinki, Finland. The telegram read: 'Dear Dad: Thanks for waiting around for me to get born. I'm coming home with the gold medal you should have won. Your loving son, Frank.'

"His son won the gold medal in the singles' 10,000-meter canoeing event—the same event his father would have competed in."

Doing without—unless you're in an upper-income financial bracket, you're going to face tough choices: "I could get those new golf clubs I've wanted for five years, or I can get braces for my kid. . .but I can't do both."

Inconvenience—kids have an uncanny ability to need things or mess things up at the most inopportune times.

Sleeplessness—sure, you can put your kid on a schedule (or try to), but even if she sleeps through the night, *you'll* never quite sleep the same deep way, knowing there's a precious life in the next room who relies totally on you (and what about when that child grows up to drive and date, etc.?).

Havoc on your body—moms, that child first grows *inside* you, and then comes *out of* you, which, if you think about it, is like something out of the *Aliens* movie series; dads, your kids will view you as the living jungle gym. In other words, get out the Ben-Gay®!

Career time-out—the evidence is slowly accumulating that kids need a parent at home; even the best child care is far inferior to the nurturing a biological mom and/or dad can provide. One of you needs to be home— *at least* during your children's preschool years. Consider the sober words of actress Katharine Hepburn:

> "I'm not sure if any woman can successfully pursue a career and be a mother at the same time. The trouble with women today is that they want everything. But no one can have it all. I haven't been handicapped by children. Nor have I handicapped children by bringing them into the world and going ahead with my career."

Emotional devastation—children have the power to break our hearts like nothing else; we ache for them as we guide them through a world that can be astonishingly cold and cruel. In time, we have to sit back and let them go. . .this is as tough as it gets.

WHO RUNS THE SHOW: THE KIDS OR THE PARENTS?

In every home there's a subtle battle for control. Or perhaps we should say there's a decision to be made about how to order the family's life.

On one end of the spectrum you have the **child-centered** home. This is a situation where the family's entire universe revolves around the children. The offspring are granted unlimited power to interrupt conversations, dictate events, disrupt established, agreed-upon schedules, and set the family agenda. For example:

Kid (whining): "Mom, I don't have the right crayon."

Parent: "It looks to me like you've got about one thousand crayons there."

Kid: "Yeah, but I don't have 'Burnt Sienna.' "

Parent: "Can't you use 'Sagebrush Sunset'? It's almost identical."

Kid: "I HATE 'Sagebrush Sunset.' Take me to the mall."

Parent: "Well, I *really* need to cook a special birthday meal for your father—oh, okay, go get in the car."

That's an exaggerated example, but many parents run themselves ragged trying to cater to every whim their kids have. And so Junior's junior league out-of-town soccer game (one of ten for the season, and one the coach impulsively added after practice last night) has the power to cancel the family's involvement in an important church event or a planned family getaway. Over time, the kid (as if he needs this not-so-subtle message) begins to think, "I really AM the center of the universe! Life revolves around ME!"

The other extreme is the **parent-centered** home. This is almost a throwback to the era of "children should be seen and not heard." The parents in such families continue to do pretty much whatever they did *before* children. The kids are expected to come along quietly for the ride while the parents indulge *their* own selfish desires. For example:

Kid (whining): "Dad, I really *don't* want to go again this weekend."
Parent (shocked): "Not go!? What? But I thought you *loved* Civil War reenactments!"
Kid: "No, Dad, actually I don't. *You* do. And, well, I just think maybe it would be nice to stay home one weekend a month and be with my friends."
Parent (hurt, yelling into the kitchen): "Honey, are you hearing this?!"

Obviously, this is an unhealthy extreme too. A big part of family life is learning to sacrifice and share and defer to each other.

In short, there are flaws with making kids the focus of family life, just as it's unhealthy to order family life around parental whims. The goal should be a **God-centered** home. This means:

Seeking His glory
Submitting to His authority
Determining to please Him
Surrendering to His plan and purposes
Living according to His revealed will (as found in the Bible)

Want to have a healthy, happy home? There's an old saying that some find cheesy, but many others have found quite helpful:

JOY is the result of putting **J**esus first, **O**thers second, and **Y**ourself third.

THE BLESSINGS AND CHALLENGES OF PARENTING

WOULD YOU LIKE FRIES WITH THAT NEWBORN, SIR?

It's really scary to realize that the average sixteen-year-old worker in the average fast-food restaurant likely has had more formal and detailed training in *how to cook french fries* than the typical new parents get in how to rear their children.

Why is that? Why is it that to get a driver's license you first have to pass both a written test and an on-the-road exam? How come in many states you can't get a gun permit until you first take a firearms safety course? What's behind the regulation that before you can enroll and begin taking classes at many private colleges, you first have to attend a comprehensive orientation session?

The reason for such rigorous restrictions and requirements is that preparatory training is a good thing. "Learning the ropes" not only pre-vents needless accidents and tragedies, it also enhances one's whole experience (whether you're talking about driving, gun ownership, college life. . .or parenting).

Now, don't freak out. There's not going to be a test over the material in this book. But the goal here *is* to give you a crash course in what to expect. The more you know going in, the more positive your experience, and the less likelihood of you making preventable mistakes.

So what **are** some of the blessings and challenges of parenting?

THE BLESSINGS OF PARENTING

- Another deduction on your tax return!

- Lots of new baby and new parent gifts (this usually includes some pampering by friends and family)

- An opportunity to see a whole new side of your husband or wife ("I've never seen him cry! It was SO sweet!")

Ancient Jewish Proverb

"When you teach your son, you teach your son's son."
—The Talmud

WOW!

- A growing appreciation for the sacrifices your own parents made for you (Though humbling, maybe even convicting, this **is** a blessing and can lead to meaningful conversations and deeper relationships with your folks!)

- Built-in accountability ("Daddy, if the speed limit is 70, why are you going 83?")

- Laughter (It's true: Kids say—and do—the most unpredictable things! "Mom, can I help Dad fix the flat? I know all the words.")

- The promise that Christ is with you (Matthew 28:20; Hebrews 13:5) and that His grace is sufficient for whatever situation you might face (2 Corinthians 12:9–10)

- The opportunity to impact the future

THE CHALLENGES OF PARENTING

Physical

Make no mistake—parenting can flat wear you out. There's usually at least some initial sleeplessness involved. Also, childbirth and breast-feeding tend to take their toll on the body (we're speaking primarily to women here; *Clues for Clueless* does not advocate *paternal* nursing).

To be sure, some Hollywood starlets with personal trainers and nannies and full-time assistants are back in spandex and looking like a million bucks one month after delivery, but it's probably unwise for you to count on a similar experience (though you *can* get back in shape with determined effort).

Emotional

Feelings of helplessness. A sense of being overwhelmed. Confusion. Fears (rational and irrational). Frustrations. Postpartum depression. Any or all of these can strike (and sometimes are often directly tied to physical exhaustion). The best remedy for most of these symptoms is deep involvement with a loving, supportive family (and church family). Refuse to let yourself get isolated!

It's interesting that in childbirth, many young, new parents report experiencing a kind of death. That is, they realize they've just said good-bye to a kind of footloose and carefree chapter of life, and they've said hello to a new phase of responsibility.

This "nostalgic" feeling is somewhat similar to what many feel at their high school graduation, only instead of your principal presenting you a diploma stating you passed the required course work, it's a hospital staff member handing you a squirming little *person* and a bill stating you owe eleven million bucks.

Financial

Okay. So we exaggerated. It's not THAT expensive. There *are* ways to live cheaply—even with a large family. Check at your local library for *The Tightwad Gazette* series of books. Some of the tips are a bit extreme ("How to make delicious soups out of everyday grass clippings"—just kidding!), but others are really economical and sensible.

Spiritual

The challenge is to be a godly parent. You want to model for your children what it means to know and love God. You want to teach them the Christian faith. This means you can't be stagnant in your own walk with God. You can't pretend to be something you're not. Even little kids can see right through a hypocritical faith that consists of words only. In some ways, this is really less a challenge and more a blessing.

Mental

You'll face an array of decisions, a whole spectrum of tough choices. You'll have to sort through boatloads of advice (including all that's in this book). Please don't be like some new parents who are so insecure they feel pressured to implement every idea that others suggest. If you don't feel right heaving your eight-month-old into a swimming pool with all the other "water babies," don't do it!

Use common sense. Find one or two older, wiser parents you respect and let them serve as an occasional sounding board. Pray continually. Read widely. Evaluate critically. But in the end, you're the one who's got to answer to God, so make decisions you feel right about.

PARENTING, THE "CHALLENGING BLESSING"

Is it more a blessing or a challenge? It's both! It's a challenging blessing. Having kids forces you to keep growing and stay on your toes. Each stage is preparation for the next. For example, pregnancy is hard, but at least the baby is confined, and you can still do pretty much what you did before. The infancy stage has its great challenges, but at least newborns can't crawl under the sink and drink drain cleaner. Toddlers are demanding, but at least they don't play the elaborate mind games that teenagers play. Do you see the point? The whole process has been brilliantly and graciously designed by God to let you gradually grow in your role as parents.

Sit back (but not too far back), relax (but not too much), and enjoy the ride!

KEEPING A UNITED FRONT AS PARENTS

THE AMAZING ABILITIES OF CHILDREN

Children come into this world with special, innate abilities such as:

- Knowing when (and what angle at which) to "spit up" so as to cause the most damage to "dry clean only" clothing and fine sofa upholstry,

- Knowing exactly where the most dangerous chemicals are stored

- Knowing when to time the acquisition of viruses and ear infections so as to cancel preplanned, "fun" getaways

WOW!

Wise Ole Ben Franklin

On the eve of the Revolutionary War, Benjamin Franklin supposedly stood and warned a bickering, divided Congress:

"Gentlemen, we must hang together, or we shall most assuredly hang separately."

If you're contemplating preganancy, don't worry. You've got lots of time to reach a consensus on all the important issues. If you're already "in the family way" as they used to say on "The Waltons" (i.e., pregnant), you've still got plenty of time to come up with a battle plan. Even if you've got a newborn, he/she is going to be napping lots, not to mention being immobile, giving you ample opportunities to put your heads together.

- Being able to memorize large numbers of commercials (especially sugary cereal ads) and then repeat them verbatim in the grocery store—in the form of a loud, whining chant
- Being able to "divide and conquer" Mom and Dad

STICKING TOGETHER

In short, to form a united front, you'll need to come to an agreement on the following child-rearing issues.
- Discipline (how, when, why, etc.)
- Diet (especially if one parent is a health-food fanatic and the other is a junk-food junkie)
- Schooling (public, private, Christian, homeschooling)
- Church involvement (especially if you come from different religious backgrounds)
- The sharing of tasks (diapering, feeding, etc.)
- Child care requirements

Have these discussions and reach some mutually agreeable solutions. The failure to do so could mean that sweet, innocent little "angel" in the crib eventually has the both of you for breakfast!

SECTION 3
WHAT EVERY FAMILY NEEDS

PARENTS WHO ARE INVOLVED

Not long ago, a prominent actress appreared on a late-night talk show to discuss her new television series. She talked excitedly about this new chapter in her career, and then, after a commercial break, the host casually asked about her recent adoption of an infant son.

Her response was rather disturbing. In essence, she admitted she had done pretty much everything else in life except "the parenting thing." And so she had concluded it was probably time to "get a kid."

Hopefully she was only joking as she made parenthood sound like something on the level of taking a vacation or buying a new

CATCH A CLUE

Scouting Report

In baseball (as well as most every other sport) players and coaches carefully and exhaustively scout the opposing teams. They watch films and chart the tendencies of individual players until they can tell you with surprising accuracy what a certain batter is likely to do when behind in the count, or what play an offense will run on first and five.

In a similar way, good parents become students of their own children. From the earliest days they begin carefully observing each child's personality traits, strengths, weaknesses, quirks, and tendencies. Mentally charting this information can help parents steer clear of avoidable negative incidents and can enhance the overall family experience.

Make it your goal to huddle with your spouse at least monthly and compare notes on the kids. Such briefing and planning sessions are invaluable in parenting.

appliance for the home. But this much is true. This celebrity and her actor husband recently divorced, leaving one to wonder: How is her young son doing? Granted, the kid probably has every material advantage in the world, but what about his emotional needs? Are they being met?

The subject we want to explore in this chapter is the whole notion of parental involvement. What's healthy and what's not?

1. Physical Involvement

Kids need your physical presence, sure. But not only that. They also crave lots of physical *contact*. So. . .hug them. Hold hands with them. Kiss them. Often! Lie in bed nightly and snuggle with them. This is a job not only for moms, but also for dads. It applies not only to little girls, but also to little boys. Dads,

Making Memories

"You never know when you're making a memory."
—Rickie Lee Jones, "Young Blood"

DON'T FORGET

as your boys grow into the toddler stage and beyond, wrestle with them on the living room floor. As you grunt and snarl and make cool noises, you are bonding and connecting with them in mysterious ways. Give piggyback rides and high fives. Every loving touch is an investment that will pay big dividends someday.

2. Emotional Involvement

Every astute person knows it's possible to be with someone, but not actually be "with" them! Fight the "distraction monster" in dealing with your children. Look your kids in the eyes. (Something about this simple act has the power to fill their emotional tanks.) Smile at them. Focus your full attention on them. Ask them questions. Encourage them to talk about feelings, dreams, and desires. Then *listen* when they respond. When they're young, such conversations will revolve around simple, concrete issues like skinned knees and ice cream and growing up to be a fireman or a dancer. If you establish the lines of communication and work at building an emotional connection when they are young, as they mature, you'll hear them verbalizing more abstract grown-up thoughts—fears about acceptance, struggles with people and situations, questions about love and faith and the other mysteries of life.

3. Spiritual Involvement

We'll say more about this in an upcoming chapter,

WIDE ANGLE

Wanted: Time

According to a 1999 survey by the Barna Research Group, the average teenager spends less than two hours per week, cumulatively, in significant interaction with his or her father.

The classic movie musical features a song called "Sunrise, Sunset" in which Tevye, the Jewish father of a large Russian family of girls, reminisces wistfully as one of his daughters prepares to marry and move away. This nostalgic montage is a shameless tearjerker of a scene, but it accurately depicts the brevity of the parenting process.

Our children will come and go in a blink of an eye. Their time under our roof and under our care will pass in a flash. God help us to savor the brief moments we will have them. May we use it wisely. May we be careful to keep our priorities straight. And may our involvement in their lives be such today that when we get to the place where Tevye sang "swiftly flow the years," we will look back with few regrets.

It's a cold, cruel, "dog eat dog" world out there. However, our kids can not only survive, but thrive if they have deeply involved parents who are committed to gently guide and faithfully rear them.

but your children need your guidance and example in learning about

God. Pray with them. (There's a good bit of truth in the old cliché
that "The family that prays together stays together.") Read Bible stories
with them. Attend church
together. The tendency among
many parents is to delegate
this responsibility to the
Sunday school or youth group.
But that isn't what God envi-
sioned for parents (see
Deuteronomy
6:1–9 and Ephesians 6:4).

Attention Please

"The greatest gift you can give another is the purity of your attention."

—**Richard Moss, M.D.**

SIGNS OF UNHEALTHY PARENTAL INVOLVEMENT

It's time to examine your parenting habits when. . .

- You find yourself missing a lot of important events and dates in the life of your child.
- You don't have a clue about your child(ren)'s strengths and weaknesses, likes and dislikes.
- You find yourself making every decision for your child (even when he/she is older).
- You feel an obsessive need to hover protectively over your children.
- You go for days without any meaningful interaction with your child(ren).
- You don't know who your kids' friends are.
- Your children feel a greater attachment to child-care providers than to you.
- Your kids spend a lot of time watching TV without supervision.

QUALITY VS. QUANTITY TIME TOGETHER

A BIT OF DOMESTIC HISTORY...

In the old days (i.e., before the Industrial Revolution), most people lived in rural, agrarian settings (i.e., on farms). The norm then was extended families (i.e., your grandparents and maybe a few aunts, uncles, and cousins too) all living—together!—under one roof. Life was hard (i.e., really difficult). People (i.e., men, women, and even young children) worked like dogs—together!—from sunup to sundown. Leisure options as we know them (i.e., separate his/her vacations, summer camp for the kids, parental getaways to a nearby B&B or to Hilton Head) did not exist. So, for fun—after milking the cows, picking a few bales of cotton, and shooting a couple of buffalo for tomorrow's lunch—men got drunk and into fistfights—together!—women made quilts—together!—and kids jumped out of the nearest hayloft or went swimming in the crick (i.e., the creek)—also together!

The key concept to grasp here is "together." In the old days families spent much more time together than they do now. But along came the aforementioned Industrial Revolution and suddenly everything changed. Fathers started going off to work long hours in factories, which meant families were forced to relocate from the country into large urban areas, which meant leaving some of the extended family behind for all the stresses of city life. In some cases, even the women and children worked. The end result was that families had less time together.

By and large this trend continued through the twentieth century. And in the 60s and 70s when women began entering the work force in droves, families faced an even greater crisis. Soon we began hearing about "latchkey" children, and before long the phrase "quality time" became popular.

The idea of quality time. . .

The notion of quality time sounds reasonable enough. A parent basically says, "Since I can't spend a great *quantity* of time with my children (because of my work and other priorities and interests), I will be sure to spend *at least a few minutes* with them—and I'll do everything I can to make sure that time is *quality*." At the core of this idea stands a conscience troubled (at least a little) by guilt, a parent desperate to avoid the charge of being indifferent or inattentive.

CATCH A CLUE

How Do You Create Quality Time?

Jay Kesler, former president of Youth for Christ, once gave an excellent analogy about the need for quantity time. He talked of his experience of watching a short clip from an action movie. Only a few seconds long, the scene was tense and exciting. The filmmaker's skill was obvious.

Afterward the man revealed to Dr. Kesler that in order to get that short piece of high-quality footage, he first had to spend many days shooting hundreds and hundreds of feet of film. Not until he had logged countless hours filming and even more time with all his reels in the editing room (leaving lots of worthless footage on the cutting room floor) did he emerge with something high quality.

The point? It's quantity time that provides the raw material for quality time.

The inherent flaw. . .

The problem with trying to schedule *quality* time with your kids is that we cannot possibly dictate when our kids are going to be sweet and cooperative and in the mood for meaningful connection: "Johnny, stop crying this instant! You're wasting our fifteen minutes of quality time!!"

It's wonderful when a father makes the special effort every Monday night to take his twelve-year-old on a "Daddy-Daughter Date." But if that two hours together is pretty much all the interaction he and she have in a given week, what happens if she's not in the mood to open up or converse?

The simple fact is that we parents can't know when our children are going to need a shoulder to cry on or an ear to confide in. We can't plan for "breakthrough moments," nor can we pick and choose the times they will want to talk meaningfully about important issues. And that's why parenting also requires quantity time. We have to be there for them, ready at any and all hours of the day. If we're not, they'll seek out someone else—a friend, a teacher, a neighbor, a talk show host, etc.—to get their emotional and relational needs met. And God help us all if that person or group imparts the wrong values.

WOW!

MIA

"As a nation, we are racked by youth violence, overrun by gangs, guns, and drugs. The great majority of youthful offenders are male, most without fathers involved in their lives in any useful way. Many have never even met their fathers.

"What's become of the fathers of these boys? Where are they? Well, I can tell you where they're not. They're not at PTA meetings or piano recitals. They're not teaching Sunday school. You won't find them in the pediatrician's office, holding a sick child. You won't even see them in juvenile court, standing next to Junior as he awaits sentencing for burglary or assault. You might see a few of them in the supermarket, but not many. You will see a lot of women in these places—mothers and grandmothers—but you won't see many fathers.

"Of course there are men who do spend time with children. These are the real men of America, the ones holding society together. Every one of them is worth a dozen investment bankers, a boardroom full of corporate executives, and all of the lawmakers west of the Mississippi."

—**Christopher Bacorn, a Texas psychologist, writing in *Newsweek*, 12/7/92**

QUALITY AND QUANTITY...
THE BALANCED APPROACH

Mark Twain once warned: "We are always too busy for our children; we never give them the time or interest they deserve. We lavish gifts upon them; but the most precious gift—our personal association, which means so much to them, we give grudgingly."

Ouch! As a parent, be there for your kids. They want your presence more than your presents. Change your priorities if they're not right. Adopt

Here's the Answer

"Child rearing is not some mysterious process. At the heart of the matter is time, huge amounts of it, freely given."
—Sylvia Ann Hewlett and Cornel West, *The War Against Parents*

THE BOTTOM LINE

an "open door"/twenty-four-hour access policy. Institute a family night. Take your kids on dates. Do chores and projects as a family. Invite children to ride with you when you're running errands.

You can never be sure when a "magical moment of connection" is going to happen. But most likely it will come at a time and place you least expect it.

A "SAFE" HOME

Most new parents go all out in attempting to "childproof" their homes. The idea here is to get down (literally!) on the creeper's/toddler's level and look exhaustively for potential hazards—low electrical outlets, unprotected cabinets containing cleaning supplies or other poisons, accessible medicine chests, enticing staircases, drawers with knives and other sharp objects, firearms, etc.

Once this sweeping inspection is complete, certain items are moved out of reach and necessary safeguards are purchased and put into place. Cleaners and prescriptions must have childproof caps. Protective plugs are inserted into all electrical outlets. Safety gates are installed to prevent access to dangerous staircases. Cabinet clasps or locks make hazardous drawers off-limits. Poison Control phone numbers are posted prominently on the refrigerator. Smoke alarms are checked with careful vigilance. For some parents, the arrival of a new child can also be the incentive for installing a burglar alarm, purchasing extra fire extinguishers, utilizing VCR guards, doing lead and radon testing, even learning infant CPR.

Why the great fuss? Because good parents care deeply about the physical health of their children. And rightly so! However, it's not enough to be concerned only for physical safety in your home; you must also be concerned about the emotional and spiritual well-being of your children. Another kind of safeguarding is necessary to insure that the emotional/spiritual atmosphere in your home is conducive to health and growth.

BUILDING A "SAFE" HOME

Home sweet home. There's no place like home. I'll be home for Christmas. Home is where you hang your hat.

Home.

What an emotionally charged term! Home is the place where our earliest and most vivid memories are made—either good or bad remembrances. Home is where, if we're lucky, we find unconditional love and constant support and someone who still believes in us, though everyone else has turned away. Home is meant to function as a kind of life raft for those dark and desperate times when the storms of life threaten to take us under. Home is supposed to be the one place we can run to when the world beats us up.

Clearly, homes are meant to be more than sterile places where our children sleep soundly and eat healthily and are kept from sticking their fingers into light sockets. On a grander scale, the goal for parents should be to create a place of all-around nourishment and warmth. The home should be, variously, an outpatient clinic or hospital, a spa, a domestic pep rally, a fortress, a rest stop, a filling station, a support group, the ultimate hospitality suite, an emotional oasis where weary, discouraged family members can find refreshment and rest and replenishment for their souls.

So how do we create such an environment? How can we make our homes "safe" in ways that transcend the mere physical?

GUARD WHAT COMES INTO YOUR HOME

If you knew that the city was pumping polluted water into your house, you'd fly into action immediately. You'd move heaven and Earth (if possible) to restrict the toxic H_2O and to see to it that your supply of pure drinking water was restored. The same is true if electrical surges started blowing your fuses and frying your electronic equipment.

Question: If we're so concerned about physical safety, shouldn't we be vigilant also about the emotional and spiritual environment in our homes?

What kinds of images and words enter your home via network television and cable? Why is it that we'd never even think of inviting strangers into our homes to have sex on the family room floor, but we'll watch strangers do that on our family room television set?

What about the Internet? Do you have child safeguards and filters in place? If not, and if your kids have access to this amazing technology, they may be in danger right there in your own home!

What kinds of magazines do you subscribe to? Is this an avenue for unbiblical, worldly ideas and values to routinely enter your home?

What about video rentals? Are you careful to forbid erotic and violent (or even marginally questionable) tapes from your VCR? Shouldn't our homes be at least one place where our minds are safe from tempting and disturbing images?

GUARD WHAT HAPPENS INSIDE YOUR HOME

- **The attitudes you display**

  Is your home a place of tension and conflict? Is there an underlying friction that threatens to erupt? Is there an atmosphere of bitterness, envy, anxiety, prejudice, or worldliness? Again, it's commendable to protect your children from the poisonous cleaners under the sink, but what are you doing to protect them from poisonous, destructive attitudes?

It is as we walk in the power of the Holy Spirit (Ephesians 5:18; Galatians 5:22–23) that we find God producing within us qualities like joy, acceptance, forgiveness, respect, contentment, and peace.

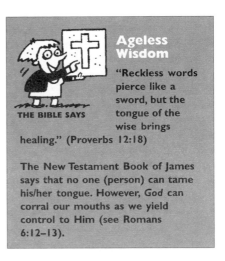

Ageless Wisdom

THE BIBLE SAYS

"**Reckless words pierce like a sword, but the tongue of the wise brings healing.**" (Proverbs 12:18)

The New Testament Book of James says that no one (person) can tame his/her tongue. However, God can corral our mouths as we yield control to Him (see Romans 6:12–13).

• *The words you use*

How do you communicate? Is there an ever-present sense of exasperation and contempt in your tone? Are you sarcastic and cutting in your remarks to family members? Do you belittle your spouse or children in confronting or correcting them? Those kinds of verbal practices don't exactly produce an "emotionally safe" home.

• *The examples you set*

It's been said that in child rearing more is caught than is taught. In other words, our nonverbal example is more powerful than our words of instruction. Our lives speak louder than our lips.

What kind of example are you? Are you a model of gentleness and kindness? Are you doing your part to make your home a safe place? Do you relate to your spouse in such a way that your children will want to grow up to be like you or marry someone like you? Remember, we're not just trying to build "safe" homes now; we're also trying to demonstrate firsthand for our children what a God-honoring family looks like. Try to be the home where all the neighborhood kids want to be. The hope is that one day our own children will strive for the same goal.

- ## *The boundaries you set*
  Safety requires boundaries. If you have a dangerous drainpipe near your home, you'll declare that "off-limits" to your children. Or you'll put a fence around it.

  In the same way, we need to declare certain activities and practices "out of bounds." You don't have to be unnecessarily strict, but you also don't have to be timid about outlawing questionable behavior. Ironically, you may even find that neighbor children gravitate toward your home as you draw lines in the sand. This is because kids naturally and innately WANT clear boundaries. This makes them feel safe. They want to hear someone tell them "no."

SOUND FINANCIAL FOOTING

It's been said that the most common complaints among husbands and wives—as reported by marriage counselors—have to do with sex, in-laws, and money (not necessarily in that order).

Since rearing a child from birth to age eighteen can be an expensive proposition—anywhere from $85,000–$250,000 depending on whom you listen to (and, to a great degree, whether you opt for disposable diapers as opposed to cloth), it's important to make sure you have reasonably sound financial footing when you embark on the parenting journey.

1. Have a biblical perspective.

Many of our economic problems and worries are due to a fundamentally wrong attitude. It's when we embrace a "me, my, mine" mind-set that we tend to become greedy and money-obsessed. According to the Bible (Psalm 24:1; Haggai 2:8), God owns it all. Everything in the whole world is His, including your portfolio and all your possessions. He is the source of every good gift. The income you have, your possessions, your money-making potential—all of this comes from His hand. By keeping this oft-forgotten truth in mind, we tend to be less anxious, less grabby, more generous, and more thankful. When you embrace the biblical perspective, you end up trusting God more for His provision and consulting Him more often on what to do with the resources that He has given you to manage.

2. Develop a fiscal plan.

Make a preliminary budget. It's not a hard process. Sit down with your

spouse and a pad of paper. Write down all your income on one side. (This is generally not a long column!) On the other side list your current monthly expenses. (Hint: It helps to keep receipts and write down every expenditure for a month or two, so that you can accurately track where your money is going.) Once you have a clear sense of your cash flow and how much you are spending in various categories (e.g., mortgage, groceries, personal care items, subscriptions, loans, prescriptions, entertainment, etc.), then you'll have a clearer understanding of why there always seems to be too much month at the end of the money. Or you may finally see

THE BOTTOM LINE

Economic Trends for New Parents

If you're the proud parents of a newborn, you should be aware that . . .

- If current trends continue, you'll only pay about $45,000 per year to send each kid to college (Only about 25–30K more per year—each—if you send them to a private school!)
- Innovative changes in the banking industry mean you'll likely be allowed to take out low-interest forty-five-year "mortgage-type" loans for everything from school clothing to orthodontia to your son's pricey car insurance premiums!
- If those facts are worrisome, the really exciting news is that your precious little darling, upon departure for the university, will be able to purchase a new computer a hundred times faster and with perhaps a million times more memory than NASA's latest model, for—get this—only $14.95 (and that will include an invisible, roll-up 60" monitor and built-in satellite receiver for receiving intergalactic digital video mail).

Remember these excellent bits of advice the next time you almost faint at the price of a pair of tiny, adorable, baby Nikes®.

why your credit card balance seems to get larger each month.

Now, adjust your budget, bringing it in line with reality. Think hard about what your financial priorities and needs really are. Begin with the absolute necessities—tithes and offerings, taxes, loans, basic living expenses (food, shelter, clothing). Ask yourself some hard questions. Can you *really* afford to spend $150/month on baby clothing? Sure, it would be great to dress your kid completely with clothes from Baby Gap®, but the reality is you may not be able to do that on your current income (and fulfill your other obligations). Should you be giving more than $25/month to support your church? What if every member family gave only that much? Are your lofty car payments on that late-model minivan causing you to forego saving money, or worse, are they pressuring you into higher consumer debt? Yes, it's hard to discipline yourself to set aside $50/month for a college fund, but down the road don't you think you're going to need that money?

This whole budgeting, prioritizing process requires that you set some goals. Many of our financial worries are due to the fact that we have no long-term objectives. When there's no agreed-upon sense of "this is what we're trying to achieve financially" our use of money becomes impulsive and erratic. It's important for couples to talk about money, to look down the road (as much as possible) and try to foresee opportunities as well as dangers. If both of you had braces as kids, and now your seven-year-old is also snaggletoothed, the chances are good little Pat is going to need to see the orthodontist in the not-so-distant future. A wise couple will begin planning ahead for such possibilities. In the same way, if you want your kids to have the best college education possible, keeping that big dream in the forefront of your minds can give you the discipline to say no to little, wasteful, unnecessary daily purchases.

SEVEN OTHER THINGS EVERY CHILD NEEDS

Over the years certain "experts" in child development studies—under the theory that kids actually have an innate sense of what they really *need* and what is really *best* for them—have advocated that young children be allowed to pretty much run their own lives: choosing their own diet, schedule, academic course load, religious ideas, etc.

This brilliant experiment has resulted in scores of children who would gladly watch TV till their brains turn into blue putty, who eat nine pounds of sugar per day, and whose knowledge of American history is that President Clinton wore boxers, not briefs.

Indeed, ask the average child on the street (er, better make that the average young boy glued to the "boob tube" with his hand in a box of Gluco-Bits) what his seven biggest needs are and you'll get some variation of the following:

1. A massive raise in my allowance
2. A much later curfew (or the abolition of all set bedtimes)
3. More Legos®, in fact. . .
4. Every toy on every commercial on every channel on TV
5. Pizza, tacos, or burgers (and no veggies!) every day
6. My own TV/VCR/Segasontari PlayStation
7. A lifetime pass to every amusement park in North America

It's an interesting list, to be sure. And yet, it doesn't really get to the core of the issue of what kids *really* need. In addition to the qualities mentioned in the previous five chapters, here are seven crucial qualities for rearing healthy, happy kids.

1. Parents who love each other

We've said it before, but the institution of **marriage** is foundational to the institution of **family**. God introduced the former before the latter.

This means a good marriage is the prerequisite to a positive home life.

When a family has at its core a loving husband/father and wife/mother, that family is marked by a tangible sense of tranquility, stability, and joy. It functions as an oasis, as a shelter from the storm that is the world (see the chapter "A Safe Home").

It's So Basic

"The most important thing a father can do for his children is to love their mother."
—Reverend Theodore Hesburgh, past president of Notre Dame

WOW!

2. Instruction in the things of the Lord

In recent years we've seen the widespread acceptance of the idea that children should not be given any sort of religious instruction. This, so goes the theory, keeps them from being unduly indoctrinated and allows them "to make up their own minds about spiritual matters."

The poet Samuel Taylor Coleridge once encountered a man who held to this idea, and, after listening to the man expound his child-rearing ideas at length, said, "Would you like to see my garden?" The man said he would. Coleridge then took the man out to view a large plot of weeds.

"Why, this is not a garden!" the man exclaimed. "There is nothing but weeds here!"

"Well, you see," replied Coleridge, "I didn't want to infringe upon the liberty of the garden in any way. I decided to allow the garden the opportunity to express itself and choose its own production."

We cannot *make* our children believe anything. But we must at least expose them (by our examples and our words) to the truth of the gospel.

3. Discipline

Kids need firm, fixed standards and clear, understood consequences for violating those agreed-upon standards. In fact, recent studies have suggested that the best-adjusted, most confident, happiest children are those who live in homes with clear boundaries.

Consider the letter one child wrote to advice columnist Abigail Van Buren a few years ago:

"Dear Abby,

My problem is my mother. She's too lenient! After she gets angry and punishes me, she often will apologize. Why should she, when I had the punishment coming?

Mixed-Up in Cleveland"

Abby replied, "Dear Mixed-Up:

Your mother (like many others) fears you will love her less because she has punished you. (She's wrong.) No child has ever resented punishment he knew he had coming. Discipline is 'proof' of love. . . Children 'know' this. I wish more parents did."

Ann Landers, Abby's twin sister and a rival advice columnist, once said the same thing:

"Children need limits set and they WANT discipline. It makes them feel secure and valued."

4. Unconditional love and acceptance

The world's version of love is "I love you IF. . ." or "I love you BECAUSE. . ." There are always conditions attached, meaning the world's love can be rescinded if one fails to meet the criteria for love.

God's love is "I love you, PERIOD." No ifs, ands, or buts. Just the irrevocable

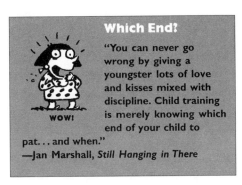

Which End?

"You can never go wrong by giving a youngster lots of love and kisses mixed with discipline. Child training is merely knowing which end of your child to pat. . . and when."

—Jan Marshall, *Still Hanging in There*

decision to seek the best for the other. It's this kind of love that gives kids confidence and enables them to blossom. They attempt great things, even in the face of possible failure, knowing they are secure in Mom and Dad's love.

Where do parents find this type of amazing love? From God Himself.

5. A solid work ethic

The so-called "builder" generation survived the Great Depression and fought World War II, resulting in a people who deeply understood the values of hard work and sacrifice. The "boomer" generation that followed was spared such hard times and grew up (thanks to their generous, hard-working parents) slightly less motivated to work hard and assume major responsibility. Then came the "busters" (commonly called "Generation X") and the "millennial kids," generations that have been, for the most part, mollycoddled, spoiled, and pampered.

Teaching our offspring how to work hard (and with excellence) is one of the greatest legacies we can give them. If we're going to succeed in this, we need to give our kids, from earliest childhood, age-appropriate responsibilities.

6. A sense of significance

God has given each of His children special gifts and abilities that, if discovered and employed, can bring Him great glory and us great fulfillment. Your kid(s) is(are) no exception. As a parent, one of your tasks is to help each child determine his/her God-given aptitudes and skills.

Some Hebrew scholars even suggest that Proverbs 22:6 can be translated, "Train up a child according to his bent" (i.e., in accordance with the way God has "wired him/her").

Could the failure of parents to obey this one command explain why so many people spend most of their lives trying to "find their place in the world"?

7. Timeless values

Dr. Albert Segal has said:

"When it comes to rearing children, every society is only twenty years away from barbarism. Twenty years is all we have to accomplish the task of civilizing the infants who are born in our midst. These savages know nothing of our language, our culture, our religion, our values, our customs. . .respect, decency, honesty. . .conventions, and manners . . . The barbarian must be tamed if civilization is to survive."

We cannot delegate this task to others. We cannot assume that our children will embrace concepts like purity, honor, and duty by osmosis.

Children must be instructed in these key concepts, and the home is the ideal classroom. Former Education Secretary William Bennett's *Book of Virtues* is a great resource to help parents teach their children timeless character qualities.

SECTION 4

NURTURE

PARENTING 101

WHAT ARE THE BASICS?

How hard can it be? You have kids and you become parents. You have basic instincts that kick in. We all live happily ever after, right?

We all know that's not true and yet we walk into parenthood surprised at how it changes our lives and, often, at how hard it is. Maybe it's because nothing we know before children can prepare us for the dailiness of it all. Maybe it's because nothing we know before children can prepare us for the wonder of it. For whatever reason, no matter how many books we've read in preparation, in walks this infant-stranger that we fall in love with and our lives are changed forever.

What are the basics of parenting? Well, basically the children. Each child goes through some relatively typical levels of development. Good parenting means meeting your children at each of their developmental stages and providing what they need to grow to the next stage. (Good parenting also means finding a way to meet your own needs as well.) The basics of parenting include every aspect of your children's lives including the physical, emotional, intellectual, social, and spiritual. You are their growing-up coach responsible for giving them the skills they need to face life, when necessary, without you. Are you up for it?

A PARENTAL MISSION STATEMENT

A mission statement is a short declaration that reveals why a person or organization exists. It should be as short and to the point as possible. It should represent the passion that makes the effort worth it.

You can find mission statements for every size of organization from fast-food restaurants to large corporations to individuals just living their lives. Why would you need a mission statement as a parent, though? Everybody knows what parents do. They raise kids.

That's true, in a sense, but no one is going to raise your kids the way you will. God put you, with your particular set of skills and gifts, in charge of a family. No matter how that family came to be in its particular configuration, if you are guardian, then you are the one called to parent. What does that really mean to you? What are your goals? Do you know specifically what you are setting about to accomplish? What do you envision twenty years down the road and how do you hope to get there?

DON'T FORGET

The Agenda

While laying plans and setting goals are important, it is just as important in parenting to be able to lay down your agenda. Life seldom goes as planned. Each child only increases the number of random and deliberate acts that can shred well-laid schedules and plans.

Remember the long-term influence you hope to have as a parent. There are many roads to that same place. When life (or your kids) throws off the whole scheme of the details of your day, trust that God is working His good though your broken agenda. Try to allow His grace to fill in the broken places so that God's agenda is accomplished through you even if your agenda is thrown away.

The more you sit back and reflect on what you are trying to accomplish as a parent, the more effective you will be. Here are a few things to consider:

- You can list your wishes for what your child will become, but you only have control over what kind of parent you become.
- As a human you will tend toward your own strengths in regards to parental style and areas of development. How will you help your child develop in the areas of your weaknesses?
- Don't forget that old expression: If you aim for nothing you'll hit it every time.
- What do you want to re-create for your kids from your own upbringing?
- What do you want to keep from re-creating for your kids from your own upbringing?
- What is your greatest passion in parenting?
- What do you most want your kids to learn?
- What kind of grown-ups do you want your kids to be?
- What kind of parents do you want your kids to be?
- What one piece of advice do you envision yourself giving your children just before their children are born?

Being able to say in one statement what you want to accomplish as a parent gives you something to come back to when the days are too long and hard and you're not sure it's worth it.

As you are thinking about what your mission is as a parent, keep in mind the difference between a mission statement and a vision statement. A vision statement can be something beyond your grasp. It is the ideal. It is your wildest dreams. Here are some examples of vision statements:

- I want to have kids that are healthy, wealthy, and wise.
- I want my children to grow up to be happy adults.
- I want to have a family that loves to be together even after I'm long gone.
- I want to be a dad who raises kids that still want to spend time with me

even when they are adults.

These are great goals. But, in reality, you can't *really* control their outcome. There will be many factors that come into the life of your family (not to mention your children having minds and wills of their own) that can undermine your idyllic visions. These are good vision statements, but they aren't enough.

A mission statement, on the other hand, is something you really can accomplish, and you can see whether you have accomplished it or not. It really has to do with what you bring to the parent-child relationship, not how you hope your kids will respond to what you bring. Here are some examples of parental mission statements:

- I want to provide an environment for my children where they will always be listened to and valued.
- I want to provide well-rounded training for my kids in financial, emotional, and spiritual growth.
- I want to provide opportunities for my kids to see a wide array of career possibilities before them.

Your mission statement is the bottom line for what you want to accomplish as a parent. What will be success for you? Don't tie it to your kids' behavior or their lifelong choices (surely by now you've learned that you can't control anyone else, even your kids, in the long run). Whom do you believe God has called you to be as a parent? Will it hold up even when the day is falling apart and your agenda is in pieces on the ground? Decide for yourself that bottom line of what you are about and hold onto it.

THE TRAPS, THE TRIVIALITIES, THE TRIUMPHS

The jungle of parenting is a precarious one. Between the possible catastrophes and the imminent trivialities there will be dangers to avoid. Between the potential power struggles and the typical family rivalries, there will be rivers to cross and mountains to climb. Accepting that can be your first step to facing whatever adversity comes without crumbling.

Deep within most of us is a belief that if we "do it right" then life will be easy. So when life isn't easy (and parenting is ripe for life not being easy), we immediately wonder what we "did wrong." Certainly we want to avoid as many mistakes as possible in parenting. That is why we read books and compare children and ask other parents how they handle the developmental hurdles their children lay before them. But in the end, life is difficult at times just because that is the nature of life. Don't make yourself and your children miserable by constantly looking for how you can make it easy. Learn

WIDE ANGLE

The Role of Children in the Home

A few generations ago children were viewed in a completely different light than they are today. When we lived in an agricultural society, the more children we had the more help we had on the farm. Also, the infant fatality rate was so high that we knew each child's life was at a great risk (think: the Waltons).

As our society progressed into an industrial age, the number of children became less of an advantage. Birth control became more popular. Children lived longer. Parents invested more of themselves in their children. Life was not so hard, so there was more room for laughter and relationships (think: the Cleavers).

As we progress into today's technological society, families have even fewer children. The life span is so much longer that it is now a life-altering tragedy when we lose a child in death. Parents feel not just proud of their children but validated by them (think: the Huxtables).

And through all this development, children have become a major economic force. Whole businesses and business strategies are built around children age twelve and under. From breakfast cereal to toys to snack foods, they are targeted in advertising at a level unimaginable just a few generations ago (think: the Simpsons).

to roll with the punches and, by doing that, teach your children to do the same thing.

Remember two things (write yourself a note and stick it in your wallet or your favorite book so you'll find it from time to time):

1. Even when you don't feel like it, you are making a difference.

    It never fails that a parent gets hemmed in by the everyday details of life that include the house, the kids, the job(s), the marriage, the dog, the neighbors, the extended family, the church, and civic responsibilities. This kind of life is a plate overflowing with collard greens and peas and no dessert in sight. Even when you don't feel like it, you are making a difference.

    Your children are learning from you no matter what frustrations you are facing. Whether you handle it well or not, include them as you deal with your own life. Are you wondering which way to turn? One day they are going to wonder the same thing. Are you regretting a decision? One day they will too. The point is, don't feel like you are only influencing your children when you are bringing glory out of the ashes. Talk to them about your mistakes and how you wish you had done it differently (after those mistakes are over and done, not as a companion to dump on). Trust God that He is laying before you the situations that your children need to see you face, as well as what you need to face to grow to be more like Him.

2. Even when it doesn't feel like it, it's worth it.

    There may not be a job that is more difficult than parenting, but there is also not a job that provides such an amazing opportunity for investment in people and in the future. A few moments of true connection between you and your child is worth a whole lot of everyday details. You are doing a good thing. Even when it doesn't feel like it, it's worth it.

    When it's all said and done—when the diplomas are earned and the new apartments away from home are furnished and the grandkids are on the way—when the children have crossed over (hopefully) and are adults, you want to be able to look back and know that you gave it your best shot. You want to know you were faithful to this call of being a mom or a dad. You want to know you were faithful to God, faithful to your kids, and faithful to yourself. Part of that process is finding a way to remember the big picture. Even when you are in the midst of a moment that holds less glory and dignity than you've ever faced (one of those moments that involve a child's bodily function as you are walking out the door on a day when your resilience is at ground zero), the big picture can pull you through.

THE BOTTOM LINE

Being a Parent Means You're Still a Person

You're reading this book because you are interested in the part of you that is a parent, the part of you that is sacrificing to help other people develop themselves. Keep in mind, though, that part of the equation is found in your own happiness and wholeness. There is no easy way to define the balance between developing yourself and helping your kids develop. But it is an important balance to struggle with. Showing your children an adult who believes a full life is possible lays a path for them to follow in being that kind of adult.

Everyone comes at this from a different perspective. Some of us have seen parents who have basically forsaken their families on the premise "I'm no help to my kids if I'm not happy myself." On the other hand, we've seen parents give up any life of their own to invest in the lives of their kids. We will bring out of our experience our own determinations about where we will land on the spectrum of being whole people and making parenting a priority. Keep working at it. Love your kids *and* love yourself. God has ordained your efforts in both regards.

HOW CHILDREN GROW

EMOTIONALLY

Children grow from no emotional control to appropriate emotional control and expression.

Babies start out with no emotional control whatsoever. And it seems that they start out with only two emotions: "I'm sleepy" and "I want. . ." As they grow they actually turn into little people with all the emotions on the spectrum: sadness, affection, happiness, excitement, depression, glee, anger, resentment, jealousy, etceteras, etceteras, etceteras. And guess who gets to be the recipient (or brunt, as the case may be) of those emotions? Well, you will be the closest target most often.

As you help your children grow emotionally, your first priority will probably be to help them learn self-control. We all know adults who have not appropriately learned self-control. There is the guy with the bad temper. There is the woman who cries at everything and expects *everyone* to cry with her. We've all seen adults whose jealousy raged out of control or whose bitterness stole years from their lives. Controlling our emotions is a lifelong effort that begins when we are children. As children we depend on our parents to validate our emotions and to help us know just how far we can go to express those emotions.

Children also grow in terms of *how* they express their emotions. We hope our kids will be emotionally transparent with the safe people in their lives. That means they will know how to choose safe people to reveal their feelings to, and when they find those safe people they will be equipped to be honest about their feelings.

How do they learn this? We first teach them this by being safe people for them to vent their feelings to. We next teach them this by validating and honoring their feelings when they express them appropriately. That means sometimes letting a child disagree with us, knowing that in the end they will still need to live within our guidelines. It means taking the time to grieve their losses and celebrate their successes with them, no matter how trivial they may seem at the time. It means not asking our children to "get over it" because we are uncomfortable watching them suffer. It means helping them realize that as bad as it feels, it will be better, and so we can hurt but not be destroyed by the pain.

SPIRITUALLY

Children grow from childish faith to faith that encounters and abides with the difficulties of life.

Who hasn't seen the beauty of children's faith? They are so trusting, so believing, that we often find our own faith encouraged by theirs. Our role is to nurture that faith as our children grow to experience the inequities and disappointments of life. We must help them understand that our faith coincides with God's eternal, consistent nature, not the convenience of life. We must help them lay the foundation for their natural faith so that as they face a life that can sometimes create doubt through difficulty they have some stronghold to return to and refuel. Here are some ideas to consider:

- We help children put roots to their faith by teaching them about our own faith.

- We help children put roots to their faith by involving them with other people of faith through church activities and friendships.
- We help children put roots to their faith by making the Word of God accessible to them.
- We help children put roots to their faith by helping them understand the relevance of God's truth to their everyday lives.
- We help children put roots to their faith by teaching them to pray, personally and daily.
- We help children put roots to their faith by sharing our own faith journeys with them, both the mountaintops and valleys.
- We help children put roots to their faith by praying for them and with them.
- We help children put roots to their faith when we put roots to our own by prioritizing our own spiritual development.

Children learn about spiritual concepts in much the same way that they learn about any concepts. They first learn the concrete truths. (God loves me. God wants me to be a helper.) Then as they grow mentally, they learn the abstract truths that flesh out our faith (salvation by grace, the nature of Jesus' substitutionary death for us on the cross). It is not our job to make our children live lives of faith. But it is our job to immerse them in an environment that will nurture their faith as it widens and expands with their understanding. In this way, we give them roots that will sustain them when we are not able to.

SOCIALLY

Children grow from awkward and inappropriate behavior to socially adept behavior and the ability to function in social settings and maintain relationships.

Babies are completely without finesse in social situations. They drool. They demand attention. They put on emotional displays that embarrass their parents and anyone around them. They remain oblivious to the looks and stares they receive. They often won't even feed themselves and, when they do, they get as much food on themselves and the floor as they do into their mouths (and even the food in their mouths they refuse to politely hide behind closed lips). Socially, babies are a wreck. That's where you step in.

It's your job as a parent to help babies turn faux pas into finesse. It's up to you to teach them to move from eating with their hands to eating with a fork. Eventually you teach them to close their mouths once the food is inside. You teach them to let someone finish speaking before they talk. You teach them to speak to guests and to share with friends. You teach them to be aware of others and their comfort. You teach them all the things that are important to you about a social situation and how to navigate through it without humiliating yourself.

On the other hand, children can have some friend-making skills that will amaze you. A playground of strangers can become a club with no grown-ups allowed in a matter of minutes. Cousins that see each other once a year at a family reunion where the adults remain remote and polite can form bonds that last throughout a lifetime.

Your role in helping your children develop socially (beside aiding and abetting their manners in every way possible) is to help them not lose their friend-making skills. As they begin to experience the relational turbulence that life can send their way (the gossip, the betrayals, the hurt feelings, the occasional rejection) they can close up. As you navigate their friendships with them, you help them not only build relationships, but also keep them. When you do this you give your child lifelong gifts.

INTELLECTUALLY

Children grow from unknowing to knowledgeable, not just about the content of books and life, but about how to learn.
For the most part children come into the world as learners. They begin grappling with the laws of nature as soon as they learn to drop the cracker off of the high chair. They experiment with the laws of cause and effect as soon as they see you laugh and connect your laughter to their actions. They learn in everything they do. What is cleverly disguised as play is their way of creating a learning lab out of anything they can move and manipulate.

With your young child, your role as parent is not so much to *teach* the child as it is to be a safety-conscious laboratory assistant and get out of the way. The learning will happen. As your child grows toward school-age, you will have more opportunities to teach him facts and skills and to give him an even more effective learning environment.

Our tendency in today's technological, computer-driven world is to be a little driven in regards to our children's intellectual environment. If we lack attentiveness in any area, it is usually not this one. So the challenges for us are not those of paying more attention or being more encouraging. The challenges for us seem to be:

1. Keeping children's development well-rounded, to include every area and not just the smarts department.

    We want so much for our children. We want them to have every advantage. Right now in our culture that seems to depend on being able to handle technology. Because of this (as well as other factors discussed in this book), we push our children scholastically from a very early age. We sometimes push to the exclusion of other appropriate priorities such as social, spiritual, and emotional development. It takes all the areas of our children's personalities and temperaments to enable them to live in excellence *and* to live in peace throughout their lives.

2. Being aware of how our children learn and encouraging them within the ways they naturally learn, rather than expecting them to learn just like we did.

We know more than ever these days about learning disabilities and learning styles. While children are less rutted into their styles of

Children Are Always on the Way Somewhere

WOW!

Children are always on the way somewhere,
Didn't you know?
From the time they enter our lives as welcomed strangers
They are struggling, straining, grappling
To get to the next place,
To do the next thing,
To overcome the next obstacle,
To face the next challenge.
You can sit back and watch, wishing things were as they were for just a bit longer,
You can even pretend to hold time still, as if you could impede their progress,
Or you can become a part of their journey,
Fanning their wings,
Wishing them well,
Celebrating their independence,
And sometimes getting to hold their hands.

learning than adults, they still tend toward a way of learning that is more comfortable for them. Observe your children. When they aren't understanding something the way you think they should be, don't just wonder what is wrong with their understanding. Also wonder how the way they are being taught could be more effective. You, more than anyone else, should know what works for your children. Try to place them in the environments where they will learn in the most effective way.

PHYSICALLY

Children grow from unskilled and undeveloped to fit and able.
Can you even put yourself in the place of a child learning to stand on his feet and walk upright? The muscle strength, the balance, the persistence, the falling, the getting back up, the starting all over—all of these things would wear any adult out in a matter of hours, if not minutes. Children are driven to use their muscles and increase their strength. What they most need from you is a safe environment in which to do it and a helping hand every so often.

The physical changes that children go through are amazing to watch. At the beginning, they seem to grow so fast that if you miss a day with them they look different. A week makes for an almost completely different child! They grow stronger. They grow taller. They grow into their head size. For some, they grow into their feet size. It can be thrilling to watch. They depend on you for the nourishment and the confidence to grow their bodies and use their bodies to grow even more.

MORAL FOUNDATIONS

RIGHT FROM WRONG

We live in an age where "right" and "wrong" are treated as relative terms, redefinable according to each situation. Because of that teaching, morality is the particular responsibility of parents. A few generations ago the school, the church, the home, and the community could all be trusted to teach a child to curb wrong impulses and make better choices.

These days there is such a variety of cultures and beliefs within the same communities. There are also heated debates between which responsibilities belong to church, which to government, and which to parents.

It is a sure thing, though, that if the home doesn't teach a child right from wrong, then the most effective avenue for learning is cut out of the child's life. Children should learn that it is right to think of the community rather than their interests. They should learn that the do's and don'ts taught them by their parents are not arbitrary controls but are based on a sense of decency and the laws of God Himself.

Right and wrong get a bad rap, though, when parents teach their children by attaching shame to them. It's one thing to communicate to a child, "Your actions are unacceptable and they are wrong." It is another thing to communicate to a child, "Because of what you have done, you are unacceptable and you are wrong." Guilt for an action turns easily into shame for a person. Perhaps this sense of shame is one of the reasons that we have strayed from letting our kids know that there is a choice to make between right and wrong. Guilt helps us do that. Shame is ineffective.

WRONG FROM RIGHT

Morality is not only knowing right from wrong, but learning the fortitude to choose right over wrong even when wrong seems much more exciting. One of the most effective ways to teach children this lesson is through your own actions. Talk to them about the situations you face in which you have to make a difficult choice between doing something the right way and doing something the easy way.

The truth is that choosing to do the right thing isn't always easy and it isn't always fun. There are not necessarily immediate rewards. This is why teaching morality without instilling a belief in God is often a futile attempt. Ultimately we do right because God asks us to do right. When we make good choices for that reason it doesn't matter as much whether we feel good choosing right. We know we have done the right thing and pleased God. Our relationship with God is intrinsically tied to our morality.

Examine your own relationship with God. Is honoring that relationship enough reason for you to choose right? Communicate that to your children. Let them know that God's friendship is important enough that they will want to do what He asks them to do.

CONSCIENCE MOLDING

We are born with the potential for understanding right from wrong. We are born with the voices that whisper to us how we should behave. Our consciences control how loudly those voices speak to us. The voice of right and wrong is like a car security alarm. We each have one and each has a sensitivity control. Our conscience is like the sensitivity control that determines just how much movement will set off the siren and red lights.

Parents mold a child's conscience from the beginning by expressing displeasure at unacceptable behavior. The child comes to understand his own conscience in stages, though. Around the age of five or six, he usually comes to realize that he can recognize the difference between right and wrong and that others can recognize it as well. Around nine years of age, it seems like the conscience of a child suddenly becomes more intense. It's at this stage that he can develop an overactive conscience or a pervading sense of guilt. Many children at this age develop some kind of nervous behaviors. Watch for these in your child. Respond to them. Remember that the child's conscience will keep him safe, but God's grace will be what ultimately brings him home. Don't bruise a child's conscience with shame and disapproval that can haunt him for a lifetime.

TEACHING INNER CHARACTER

RESPONSIBILITY

You don't have to look far to find someone—a columnist, a senator, a parent—raging about the irresponsibility of kids today. Either they are staying at home too long and living off Mom and Dad or they are destroying property (and sometimes the word *willy-nilly* creeps in here). So are kids born responsible or are they made to be responsible?

You know the answer—both. Some kids are conscientious worrywarts from the beginning. Some are carefree spirits. Some are self-focused by nature and fight with that all their lives. Nevertheless, you can help your children learn to be responsible.

Children learn responsibility by seeing it and by being given it. First, *you* must be responsible in front of your children. (Are you the worrywart, the free spirit, or the self-focused person?) Then you must give them appropriate doses of responsibility. Too much at a time won't accomplish your goal. Too little will not let them know the price of irresponsibility.

Define the chores your children are responsible for and increase their responsibilities. Remember to protect your relationship with your children by not giving them responsibilities that, should they fail in them, will affect you to the point of anger or rejection. Don't make them dust if your precious things will be at risk of being broken by your precious children. Give them the responsibilities that they are capable of and give them consequences if they are irresponsible.

INTEGRITY

Integrity is the concept that we used to call character. A person with integrity is a person who sticks to his sense of right and wrong no matter who is watching. It's the person that you know will do the right thing even if he could do the wrong thing and not get caught. What gives a child integrity? First of all, a parent with integrity. Your child sees more of your life than you'd like to think. He learns from you even when you don't know you are teaching. If he sees you cheat when you know you won't get caught, then he will learn to do the same. This is why having kids often makes us better people. It's why people often clean up their acts more while they are parenting their kids than before or after.

Explain to your children why you make the choices you do. When you correct them, address the level of integrity that they are exhibiting, not just the actions that you are evaluating. When you watch TV together talk about the characters you see and the character they exhibit. Find heroes for your child that show some integrity. Protect your children (as much as is possible) from peers who find joy in cheating and deceiving. Be honest with your kids about why you don't want them to have that influence. (It's hard enough in this world, with our sinful hearts, to do the right thing; we need our friends to make it easier, not harder.)

TEACHING RESPECT FOR AUTHORITY

How do you talk about your pastor around the dinner table? What do you do when you are driving with your child and a policeman comes into view? How much do you respect the authorities in your life? How much do you want to be respected as an authority?

In a world where we have to teach children not to trust every adult, teaching respect for authority can be a difficult thing. Remember that you are teaching respect for positions of authority. We should speak respectfully to government officials, to pastors, to judges, and to police officers. We should respect their positions. As your children grow, they can learn to make that distinction. When you come across a person who is in a position of authority, take the opportunity to explain to your kids that you want to show respect to that position. (This might do you some favors when you hit those adolescent years when every shred of authority is up for grabs.)

TEACHING LIFE SKILLS

LIFE SKILLS?

Parenting is teaching a child how to live his life on into adulthood. Parenting is teaching that child the skills he will need not just to make a living but also to face life and to cope with the life he faces.

THE ABILITY TO MAKE TOUGH CHOICES

Being able to evaluate choices and make the right ones is a skill we chase all of our lives. You can help your children be better prepared to make tough choices and decisions.

Evaluate with them the good and bad sides of decisions they are making. Give them the sense that they can figure it out; it will just take time. Teach them how to ask for advice and make sure they have access to wise adults (yes, even besides you) in their life to ask for advice from. Give them the self-confidence to trust themselves in making decisions.

Start early with laying out options for your children. When they have a practice and a party and a family gathering all scheduled at the same time, sit down and talk through their choices with them. Give them plenty of practice on choices that don't have severe consequences before you get to the ones that do. Don't pretend that they have a choice when they really don't (if you demand that they go to the family function, don't try to manipulate them into choosing that).

Give them practice at deciding on what is more important to them (not just to you) and why. These are the things that stump us about tough choices. Deciding between what we want and what others want and what seems right is a muddle of an experience. Help your child learn to be clear about what he wants even if he can't have it.

Also try to work out compromises when possible. How often in life do we feel like we have to give up one thing to have another when we might be able to have both, but with a few compromises. Ask your child to come up with some options. ("We can't watch this whole movie and go pick up your brother by 2:30 from his class. Can you think of a way we can do both?")

When you face tough decisions in life, imagine your child facing those decisions one day. What simple skills can you help him develop now that will prepare him for those big decisions that will surely come in life?

FACING CONSEQUENCES

Your child will face consequences in his life just like you do. You can't keep it from happening. In fact, if you try to keep it from happening, you'll probably make it harder on her in the long run. The lesson for you to teach your child is the same lesson God lays before us: You will not keep her from the consequences of her actions, but you will always stand by her as she faces those consequences.

Why do we often want to rescue our children from negative consequences?

- To give them another chance
- Because we think they didn't mean to do the wrong thing
- Because we don't want them to be embarrassed
- Because we don't want to be embarrassed ourselves

- Because we don't want their potential to be stunted or ruined

What do we rob our children of when we step in and intervene between their actions and their consequences?
- The faith they would have developed
- The lesson they would have learned
- The more severe consequence they may have avoided in light of the experience

The key with this life skill is the same as any other. Give your children practice at this skill before they face the big, tough situations. Let them face preschool-sized consequences as a preschooler. Give them a clear view of the fact that their actions created reactions and they are the ones responsible. Hopefully if you enable your children to face their consequences *as* they grow, they will be better able to look ahead and weigh out consequences when they are grown.

CHOOSING OTHER CAREGIVERS

NANNIES

While nannies used to be a privilege of the wealthy, rising child-care costs have pushed the use of nannies lower and lower down the economic strata. A nanny is a person who regularly cares for your child in your home. She becomes a surrogate member of the family. Usually nannies are used for children under three years old.

There are professional nannies who advertise and move from one household to the next. There are nannies who specialize in one age group and then release your child to another form of care. There are nannies who live at

CATCH A CLUE

Did You know?

Did you know that nannies are an organized profession? Not only are there nanny schools such as. . .

English Nanny & Governess School (in Ohio, no less)

Northwest Nannies Institute (NNI)

There are also professional nanny organizations such as...

International Nanny Association (INA)

Nanny News

National Association of Nannies (NAN)

Seattle Nanny Network (SNN)

your home and there are nannies who come and go as you come and go from work.

There are also *au pairs* or short-term nannies. Au pairs are usually young women who hire themselves out as nannies for the opportunity to visit another country and get to know another culture.

DAY CARE

In just one short generation, day care has become an integral part of our society. Day cares come in many forms. There are national chains. There are local day cares. There are small day cares set up in someone's residence. But the things that you should look for in a day care are pretty much the same no matter what the size or notoriety of the day care. Keep these things in mind.

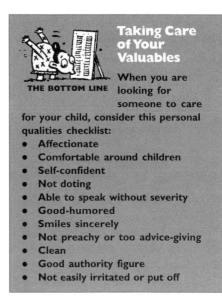

Taking Care of Your Valuables

THE BOTTOM LINE

When you are looking for someone to care for your child, consider this personal qualities checklist:

- **Affectionate**
- **Comfortable around children**
- **Self-confident**
- **Not doting**
- **Able to speak without severity**
- **Good-humored**
- **Smiles sincerely**
- **Not preachy or too advice-giving**
- **Clean**
- **Good authority figure**
- **Not easily irritated or put off**

- How many adults are in each classroom? (There should be one adult for every five children.)
- Are you welcome to stop by unannounced and check on things?
- Is there plenty of space for the children to play in?
- Are there small spaces where children can play quietly away from the group?

- Are the teachers sitting and watching or interacting with the children?
- Do the workers seem friendly?
- Do the children seem relaxed and cooperative?

BABY-SITTERS

Baby-sitters are people that you invite into your home on an as-needed basis. Baby-sitters come in all ages, but we often think of them as mid to late teenagers who are responsible enough to call you if something goes wrong, but are not old enough to have a job, car, and life of their own.

The most important trait in a baby-sitter besides a general sense of responsibility is a knack with children. It's a great idea, if you can do it, to hire the sitter to come by a few times while you are at home so that the child is familiar with the person and has seen you with the sitter.

It's also a good idea to gather some important information in a notebook so that it will be available each time the sitter comes. This will keep you from rushing

CATCH A CLUE

Flag on the Play

When you're considering any form of child care, watch out for these warning signs.

If you don't feel right about it, but you're desperate—wait.

If you can use an extended family member, but they tend to favor one of the children over the others—keep looking.

If a caregiver has loads of experience, but they are too possessive of the child and their own ideas—do another interview.

If a caregiver has a good educational background, but is fussy or uptight with children—look elsewhere.

around looking for numbers as you are getting ready. Your information should include:

- Your child's routine
- Some typical requests from your child (particularly if your child is not speaking clearly yet)
- Emergency numbers such as doctors, neighbors, and relatives
- Where to find linens and nightclothes in case there is a spill or an accident
- How to change the temperature in the house

SECTION 5
SPIRITUAL DEVELOPMENT

SPIRITUAL DEVELOPMENTS

STAGES OF GROWTH IN YOUR CHILDREN

Not too long ago, a nationwide poll was taken among parents and the overwhelming majority (something like eighty percent!) stated that their children were "above average." Never mind the fact that this is mathematically impossible. The truth of the matter is that we're convinced our kids are advanced in every way—intellectually, emotionally, socially, athletically, even spiritually.

However, as fervently as we might think this, the truth is that our children still need to be taught. They do *not* come into this world fully developed in any area, especially when it comes to the spiritual realm. As a matter of fact, the Bible states that our children (as innocent as they might appear) are born in sin. They are, to use a big theological term, depraved (and thus not "basically good"). They are innate rebels, spiritually dead, and separated from God. Consequently, their biggest need in all of life is to be saved from sin and death—by admitting their sinfulness, by accepting Christ's sacrificial death on the cross as the only sufficient payment for their sins, and by putting their trust in Him. Once they've met Jesus Christ on *His* terms, then their biggest need is to follow Christ for the rest of their lives, and through that process of loving and serving Him, to become like Him. (Reader's note: If, as a parent, *you've* never walked through this salvation process, then it is also YOUR biggest need!)

The point is that spiritual development, like any other kind of growth, is a process. And so even though you know the goal (meeting and becoming like Jesus), it's also helpful to recognize the stages most kids pass through. (Note: These are not hard-and-fast or observed in every child or always evident in the order in which they are listed.)

The "parroting" stage: Toddlers will repeat anything you say, even about God. Though she can say, "I love Jesus," it doesn't follow that she comprehends what she's saying.

The "magic" stage: God is viewed almost as a cosmic genie. His "size" and power are emphasized over almost everything else. The miracle stories of Jesus evoke childlike wonder.

The "fear" stage: As young children try to process facts about eternity and death and heaven and hell and the devil, they may go through a very normal period in which they act almost afraid of God. They may even make statements like "I don't want to go to heaven." Do not panic!

The "pleasing" stage: Many older children learn that it pleases their parents to hear them make positive statements about Jesus and God and the Bible. Thus, they will often demonstrate a great interest in spiritual things. Parents should certainly encourage this, while realizing that it does not necessarily indicate the presence of true faith.

The "questioning" stage: Preadolescents and teenagers begin asking hard questions as they bump up against the hard realities of life. The death of a friend, a news report about a terrible famine or disaster, a minister's statement that a billion Muslims are "lost"—any such event can precipitate a scary "faith crisis" in your child. This is a tough but necessary stage of life in which young adults wrestle with the implications of their faith.

The "owning one's own faith" stage: This is where a person no longer believes because his parents do or because her youth pastor told her to, but because he/she has examined the facts and has determined that the gospel is true. This, not a handed-down or borrowed faith, is the goal.

FOSTERING SPIRITUAL GROWTH

How do parents "foster spiritual growth" in their kids? That sounds like a hard thing, like perhaps one might need a seminary degree to *really* do it right.

Not so. There are no guarantees, but there are some very simple things you can do.

1. Pray.

There's probably nothing in the world more profound or powerful in the parenting process than our faithful intercession for our kids. Prayer is a great mystery. Why and how does God use it? Who can say, really? But as one man quipped, "When I don't pray, not much happens; when I do pray, wild things happen!"

What's the Secret?

THE BOTTOM LINE

"There is no easy, push-button method of teaching your children the truth about God, and there is no romantic, smooth, undisturbed section of time in which to do it! Just as life is not made of neat little packages of time for other things, so this matter of having good intentions, but always being disturbed in scheduling the 'right time' for Bible reading, prayer, discussion, reading Bible storybooks, or answering questions, can go on so long that the precious years are gone! What God put in Deuteronomy cannot be improved upon as to 'when'—and that is when you are sitting together, getting ready for bed, walking, and so on. This means time is meant to be spent together."
—**Edith Schaeffer,** *What Is a Family?*

Many parents erroneously "claim" Proverbs 22:6 as a "promise" from

God that if they'll force-feed their kids the Bible and faithfully drag them to church, then they're guaranteed a crop of Christian children who will love and serve God.

It's a nice thought. Unfortunately that's not the intent of this verse. The book of Proverbs is wisdom literature. In other words, the proverbs aren't intended to be promises; rather they are Solomon's generally true observations about life. And life, as we all know from experience, is full of exceptions.

The point? Do all you can to encourage your kids to follow God, but then pray like crazy!

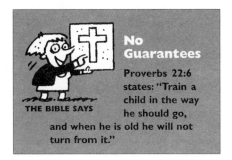

No Guarantees

THE BIBLE SAYS

Proverbs 22:6 states: "Train a child in the way he should go, and when he is old he will not turn from it."

2. Have a plan.

You don't have to pull out an overhead projector and outline the book of Romans for your toddler or give your first grader a syllabus for his spiritual life, but it couldn't hurt to sit down with your spouse and sketch out a flexible plan. For example, you might decide to read through the Bible (an age-appropriate version) with your children every year or two. You might choose to memorize one verse a week (or month) together. You'll certainly want to pray daily with each of your kids (and not just at mealtimes!). Teach them how to share the good news about Jesus. Take older children to a Walk Thru the Bible seminar or to a *Destination 2000* conference.

3. Take advantage of teachable moments.

It's usually in the fast-food drive-thru lane or at the pool or lying in the dark together at bedtime (and not during family devotions after supper) that kids ask the really juicy questions. Be ready to turn such situations into brief opportunties for spiritual instruction.

You can even use bad examples for good results. For example, if you get angry and lose your temper, apologize and ask your kids for forgiveness (and make sure you explain to them that this is what God tells us to do in His Word).

4. Get involved in a really good church.

Don't just attend occasionally. Join, serve, give, go, worship, support. Model for your kids what commitment to a local group of believers looks like.

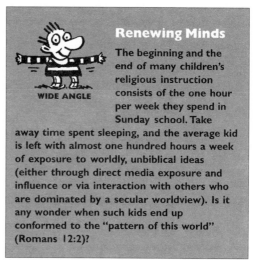

Renewing Minds

The beginning and the end of many children's religious instruction consists of the one hour per week they spend in Sunday school. Take away time spent sleeping, and the average kid is left with almost one hundred hours a week of exposure to worldly, unbiblical ideas (either through direct media exposure and influence or via interaction with others who are dominated by a secular worldview). Is it any wonder when such kids end up conformed to the "pattern of this world" (Romans 12:2)?

WIDE ANGLE

5. Utilize age-appropriate books, stories, and videos.

Pay a visit to your local Christian bookstore. There are a lot of good resources available for helping your children grow in their faith. (Beware! There is also a lot of junk and a lot of silly fads!) Realize that even some older "secular" children's literature like *The Chronicles of Narnia*, the stories of Hans Christian Andersen, and old classics like *Pinnochio* and *The Little Mermaid* (**not** the Disney versions) can help awaken your child's moral imagination.

MODELING CHRISTIANITY

Dad (an enormous bite of roast beef and mashed potatoes practically tumbling out his mouth): "Hey! Howf many timbes do I have to ptell you to watsch your tablef mannthers?!"

Mom (cruising about 40 mph in a 25-mph zone): "Sweetie, just because you don't agree with the rules at school, doesn't mean you have the right to ignore them!"

Mom and Dad (preparing to insert an R-rated video into the VCR): "Because we're old enough and mature enough to watch it, that's why. And you're not. Now go to bed!"

MORE IS CAUGHT THAN TAUGHT

There are few things worse in life than a person who doesn't practice what he preaches, or an individual who says, "Do as I *say*, not as I *do*."

When it comes to the spiritual nurture of our children, we must lead by clear example. We must model the truth. When our actions fail to correspond with our words, our lives take on a hollow, artificial look. Something doesn't ring true. We become inauthentic, to paraphrase one author, like travel agents describing places we've never actually been to but only read about in brochures.

The Practicum of Real Life

In his final words to the people of Israel before they entered the Promised Land (and he died), Moses gave them this solemn bit of advice:

"These commandments that I give you today are to be upon your hearts. Impress them on your children. Talk about them when you sit at home and when you walk along the road, when you lie down and when you get up. Tie them as symbols on your hands and bind them on your foreheads. Write them on the doorframes of your houses and on your gates" (Deuteronomy 6:6–9).

What Moses was describing was an integrated faith, a way of life. God (His reality and His will) were to be made part of normal everyday family interaction. The commandments were to be not only taught but lived out.

In the New Testament Christians are warned:

Little Mimics

"Children are natural mimics who end up acting just like their parents, in spite of all attempts to teach them otherwise."

—Author unknown

WOW!

"Do not merely listen to the word, and so deceive yourselves. Do what it says" (James 1:22).

PRACTICAL WAYS TO MODEL YOUR FAITH

Though the Bible is clear that we should never be showy and do religious activities merely for effect (Matthew 6:1–7), it *is* important to let our kids see that faith in Christ has real, practical implications on everyday life.

Base your life on the Scriptures. In an era when, according to the Barna Research Group, more than eighty percent(!) of teens say there are no moral absolute truths or definitive realities, your children need to see you turning to God's Word for direction and solace.

Have a daily devotional time. Teach your children the importance of being alone with God every day for a time of prayer and biblical meditation.

Work at having good relationships. The heart of Christianity is relating rightly to God and to others. Memorized Bible verses and "moral uprightness" don't mean much if you and your spouse fight constantly or if you treat waitresses and bank clerks rudely.

Be vitally involved in a local church. Author/psychiatrist/Christian Paul Tournier once said, "There are two things one cannot do alone. One is be married. The other is be a Christian." Your kids need to grasp the essential truth that the New Testament teaches a community-based faith, not a privatized spirituality.

Practice hospitality and generosity. How easy it is to twist the gospel around into a belief system where we're the point, and where the goal is to accumulate blessing after blessing. And how wrong! The heart of Christianity

CATCH A CLUE

Model It Well

"Every father should remember that one day his children will follow his example instead of his advice."
—Author unknown

is being other-centered and reaching out to bless those around us. Let your kids see you (and join in) ministering to those who are hurting.

Be a witness. At appropriate times, as the Spirit gives opportunities, let your kids see you articulating your faith with friends, neighbors, and family members. If they never see you sharing the gospel with others, they will obviously conclude this is not an important mission.

GROWING AS A FAMILY

Someone somewhere once uttered the immortal line: "When the horse is dead, get off."

Meaning, your *Clues for the Clueless* editorial team doesn't want to belabor the point here. We're guessing you've read the previous chapters and are in agreement that spiritual growth is a critical ingredient in a healthy family life. Parents need to be walking faithfully with God and they need to be committed to helping their children come to know and serve the Lord.

There's not a lot more we can say about this process. But we can close with some great, practical ideas for "growing (spiritually) as a family":

It's Like Planting

WOW!

"In planting beans the old practice was to put three in each hole: one for the worm, one for the crow, and one to live and produce the crop. In teaching children, we must give line upon line, and precept upon precept, repeating the truth which we would inculcate, till it becomes impossible for the child to forget it.

"We may well give the lesson once, expecting the child's frail memory to lose it; twice, reckoning that the devil, like an ill bird, will steal it; thrice, hoping that it will take root downward, and bring forth upward to the glory of God."
—**Charles Haddon Spurgeon**

1. Dads—lead the way. Like it or not, God expects you to set the pace in your home. If you're not growing, your wife and children will suffer. Get in a men's Bible study or discipleship group. As you go, so goes the rest of the family.

2. Mom and Dad—pray together and read the Scriptures together. . .DAILY. A simple twenty-minute time of interaction with God can do more for your marriage and spiritual health than you can possibly imagine!

3. Go to a Christian camp together. A growing number of conference centers now offers week-long experiences for the whole family. You'll have fun and be challenged from the Word of God. You can do an Internet search for details and up-to-date information.

4. Support a missionary together. Get the whole family involved in praying and giving and writing notes (or E-mails) of encouragement.

5. Go on a short-term missions trip together. Use your vacation. Get out of your comfort zone (i.e., rut). Step out in faith and get your hands dirty for God. You'll never be the same. One kid who just got back from a seventeen-day mission trip to Malawi, Africa ranked the experience as far, far superior to any family vacation she had ever taken!

6. Read Christian classics together. *The Chronicles of Narnia*, missionary biographies, as well as books like *The Pilgrim's Progress* and *In His Steps* can make a profound difference.

7. Eat meals together. Sadly, this practice is on the "endangered species" list of family activities. Turn off the TV; don't be in a rush. Instead, talk about life (and about how God and His truth relate to the day's events). Listen to one another and encourage each other to keep following Jesus.

SECTION 6
DISCIPLINE

PUNISHMENT VS. DISCIPLINE

What exactly do you mean by "punishment"?

Punishment is the negative consequence that follows when someone breaks a rule. That rule might originate from parents, God, nature, life in general, or personal ethics—nevertheless, breaking the rule brings punishment. That punishment, hopefully, serves the purpose of pointing out your error (if you didn't already notice it) and hopefully deterring you from making that error again.

Punishment has its place. When you punish children for running out in the street, they may not understand why their

WIDE ANGLE

Which Is Which?

In your opinion, which of these scenarios represents an act of mere punishment and which represents an act of discipline? Compare with the opinion of someone else in your household.

1. Jana gets a sticker every day that she makes her bed. If she gets five stickers during the week it's *sno-cones* on the weekend! If she doesn't...no treats.
2. David gets his hand smacked every time he touches the remote.
3. Jessica is sitting in the corner with her face to the wall. She'll stay there until Mom says she can come out. Why? She hit her brother.
4. Jonathan got two blue marks at preschool today. If he gets three within a day he will have to sit in time-out during recess.

What was your opinion? Well, according to the panel of armchair experts all four could be a part of discipline if there is an overall plan attached to them. As they are listed here 2 and 3 are really just punishment—a specific consequence for a specific action.

actions were foolish, but they won't be as prone to do it again. Punishment, therefore, helps a parent particularly when a child is too young to understand all the "whys" of his actions.

But for this same reason, punishment alone is not enough to lead a child to be a responsible adult. Children don't remain unable to reason. They grow to the point where they can understand the "whys" and the "becauses," and at that point they need more than punishment. They need guidance. They need information. They need explanations. They need the reasons and the skills to control their own behavior. Punishment alone is not enough. Kids need discipline.

How is discipline different?

Discipline, from a parent to a child, is much more far-reaching than punishment. Punishment addresses an action. Discipline addresses a lifestyle. Punishment deals with one situation. Discipline deals with the child's ability to control himself, to work within guidelines, to function in a family and in society.

When you punish a child for leaving his bike in the driveway, you give him a single consequence to avoid that will hopefully deter him from doing it again. On the other hand, in disciplining your child, you deal with the big picture. That picture includes his role in the family and his responsibilities for his possessions. That picture also includes helping him understand the importance of putting his bike away for his sake, its sake, the car in the garage's sake, and his relationship with his parents' sake.

What makes discipline difficult?

Discipline takes a *lot* more work than mere punishment. Discipline is one of the top five reasons it is difficult to be a parent. Discipline is raising a kid, not just punishing disobedience. Discipline is the effort to mold a life and teach behavior, rather than just keeping a kid out of your hair and out of trouble. Discipline requires having a plan. It requires a serious undertaking in the role of a parent. Disciplining a child requires inner discipline. It's much easier to do your own thing and just correct the child when she steps out of line. Discipline requires a disciplined parent. That's work any way you look at it.

Perhaps we confuse the two because punishment is a part of discipline. Punishment is a tactic, a strategy in the overall plan that we call discipline. We also confuse them because when we talk about punishing a child we often use the word "disciplining" interchangeably with "punishing." Don't be mistaken, though; there is a significant difference.

Punishment vs. Discipline

WOW!

"I remember the first time I realized the difference between punishment and discipline. I had repeatedly asked Elisa to clean up her new toys from the playroom. I was in a hurry and was snapping at her, telling her she should know better. I was verbally punishing her for not immediately obeying me. Finally I started putting them up myself. She looked at me and said, 'How did you know where they went?' I had been so busy fussing I hadn't stopped to help her organize her space to accommodate the new toys she had gotten for her birthday. I should have been helping her learn how to put things away instead of just being concerned with a picked-up room."
—Isabel, Kearny, NE

"YOU'RE GROUNDED FOR LIFE!"

Why do we say what we don't mean when we're angry?
It doesn't really matter what the relationship is—parents to parents,
parents to kids, boss to employee, or friend to friend—when we are angry
we all say and do things we don't mean to say and do. Why? Because
strong emotion colors our perception of life. The adrenaline starts pumping. The panic rises. Everything feels more *INTENSE!*

In short, we have a harder time controlling what we say and do when
we are angry. This is why parents promise cruel and unusual punishment
at the emotional height of a confrontation, then wish they could take it
back (without reeking of inconsistency) when things calm down a bit.

Why do we say what we don't mean when we're angry? Because the
truth is, when we're angry, we usually mean it. When we are angry, we are
not looking at the whole, long-term, lifelong picture. We aren't worried
about the whole scope. When we are angry, we are just concerned with
what made us angry and the person who is responsible for that.

That doesn't pose a tremendous amount of problems when we are
lashing out at the employee at the car wash who forgot to roll up the car
window or the store clerk who wouldn't let us return the shirt that just
doesn't fit. Chances are, we won't see those people again. With our
children (or other family members), though, we live with them day in and
out. What we say in anger we will both live with for a long time. For that
reason, no matter how difficult it is to control what we say and do in anger,
we've got to give it a shot.

But does it make sense to punish when you're angry?

You are the exception if you were not punished in anger as a child. In fact, it's very easy for children to grow up believing that they would never get punished if they never made their parents "mad." Somehow that seems to makes sense.

But the reality is that punishment has to do with right and wrong, appropriate and inappropriate behavior, not with the emotional condition of the parent. That doesn't mean that parents don't get angry. You know they do! And, often, justifiably so. Children are consistently pushing the limits, which means testing the parents, which means aggravation. Parents are not required to put aside all their emotions in order to raise their kids. But there is a difference between expressing your emotions to your child and punishing your child just because she irritated you. The degree of punishment is according to the degree of the offense

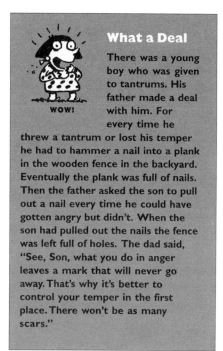

What a Deal

There was a young boy who was given to tantrums. His father made a deal with him. For every time he threw a tantrum or lost his temper he had to hammer a nail into a plank in the wooden fence in the backyard. Eventually the plank was full of nails. Then the father asked the son to pull out a nail every time he could have gotten angry but didn't. When the son had pulled out the nails the fence was left full of holes. The dad said, "See, Son, what you do in anger leaves a mark that will never go away. That's why it's better to control your temper in the first place. There won't be as many scars."

WOW!

(which shouldn't fluctuate between events), not according to the level of the parents' emotions (which could very well fluctuate hourly).

"But when I'm not angry anymore, I don't feel like carrying out the punishment." Then you need to reevaluate what your idea of discipline is.

You're teaching your children right from wrong, not how to get around their parents' moods. Either your punishment may have been unrealistic, or you might not be doing right by your kids to let it slide.

What to do to buy some time to cool off

So when you're angry and not feeling *quite* in control, you need to buy some time, get some space, slow it all down so that you can think with your logical self and not your emotions. The problem is that if you are disciplining a very young child, you know that after time passes she may not make the connection between the offense and the discipline.

Here are some ways to buy some time:

1. Walk away if the child is not in danger.
2. Put the child in a safe time-out place and sit down in a comfortable place and *breathe.*
3. Call a friend and talk it through.
4. Sit the child down across from you, but too far away to reach and count to fifteen or so, *slowly.*

DON'T FORGET

Idle Threats?

"I really couldn't believe I did it. My mom had always told me, 'Don't threaten your children with something that you are not going to do.' So, no matter how hard it was on all of us, I carried out my threats. But one day I really blew my stack and threatened them to the moon. As soon as the words were out of my mouth I regretted them. After A.J. had gone to his room, and I'm sure gratefully so, I did something I honestly had never done before. I went to him and apologized and asked his forgiveness. I know it's not what my mom would have done, but I've got to believe that if he sees I'm willing to ask his forgiveness, then maybe he'll know better how to ask mine. He still got punished, but we weren't both miserable anymore."
—Pat, Nashville, TN

APPROPRIATE FOR THE OFFENSE

Why do things get out of hand?

You have probably, at one time or another, witnessed discipline that is more harsh than necessary. Whether it is the parent who yells too loudly or the food piled too high for the "eat everything on your plate" rule, there is a real sadness to observing this kind of situation.

Part of what creates this is the element of control. When it comes to the point of doling out consequences, parents are often just trying to regain control of a situation. They are not unlike a general who is trying to gain control of a rebellious colony. If he has the opportunity for overkill to make his point, he often uses it. So it sometimes goes with parents who are making an attempt at keeping the household running and their sanity intact.

The emotion of the situation also plays into the overall picture. Sometimes the discipline that seems appropriate to meet the emotion of the situation is still too harsh to match the actual offense. If parents are momentarily separated from a child at the store, it often has as much to do with the parents' watchful eye as with the child's obedience. But the fear from that separation can send voices raising and threats descending as if the child had planned an all-out escape with underground tunnels and fake German uniforms.

Rules of thumb

There are several things to consider when you are deciding on consequences for your child's actions.

1. Intentionality. Did he mean to? Was he being malicious or was it imma-

turity, or exhaustion, or silliness?

If your child was intentionally disobeying, then restriction of some privilege is definitely on the horizon. If you've kept him out without a nap and you know he is running on empty, it might be enough to explain why his behavior was unacceptable as you put him down for a nap.

2. Danger. If the child repeats this offense how badly could she be hurt?

It might be OK to go for a few tries on "don't throw your books" but for "don't run out in the road" you want the lesson to stick the first time, if possible.

3. Amount of repetition. Is this a new lesson? Is the child at a new place of understanding?

If you've gone over this same point many times before, first of all you might consider why your communication is not working effectively. If you really do feel confident that the child is disregarding you, the punishment should be more severe. On the other hand, if you've only faced this situation a time or two before, leave some room to grow.

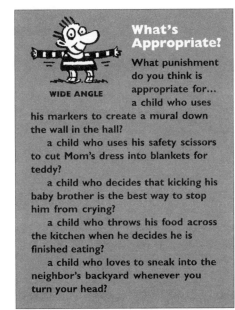

WIDE ANGLE

What's Appropriate?

What punishment do you think is appropriate for... a child who uses his markers to create a mural down the wall in the hall?

a child who uses his safety scissors to cut Mom's dress into blankets for teddy?

a child who decides that kicking his baby brother is the best way to stop him from crying?

a child who throws his food across the kitchen when he decides he is finished eating?

a child who loves to sneak into the neighbor's backyard whenever you turn your head?

SPANKING AND TIME-OUT

What is spanking about?

It was just a few short generations ago that spanking was the standard punishment for childish wrongdoing. Whether in school or at home, there was some kind of paddle handy and ready for use. A lot has changed since then. The awareness of physical abuse, the sensitivity to violence, the new crop of thinkers and writers and teachers on discipline all have worked together to communicate, "There is another way."

The proponents of spanking refer to references such as "spare the rod and spoil the child," which does *not* appear in the Bible, and many other similar references that *do* appear there. They also defer to their own upbringing: "My momma spanked me and I think I turned out OK" (a few raised eyebrows usually follow this statement).

The opponents of spanking refer to the biblical message lying beneath the cultural method: "Discipline your children, or raise rotten people." They defer to logic: "Why teach your children that things can be settled with violence?" At one time or the other we've all heard about the little boy who has hit his brother, so his father yells, "We don't hit people!" and gives him a spanking.

Spanking is about pain inflicted in association with bad behavior. The logic is that if something painful happens every time a child does a certain behavior he will eventually stop doing it. This logic is much the same as the conditioning of Pavlov's dogs, who began to salivate upon hearing bells, since for a long time they had been fed at the same time bells were rung.

Many parents who love their children and would never mistreat them still spank their children and claim it an effective practice. These parents are not abusers. They are careful not to spank in anger. Many refuse to use their hand against the child which is why they use a paddle of some sort. Nor do these parents believe that they are solving problems with violence. They aren't spanking the child to get him to make a decision or to make him learn to read. The punishment comes as a direct consequence to disobedience, not an overall fear tactic.

The dangers of spanking? It's much easier for physical punishment to become too intense when emotions are flying. Physical punishment also leaves dignity a bit less intact than restrictions (which is why

THE BOTTOM LINE

Think First

There are few absolutes when it comes to methods of discipline. The bottom line is going to be what is effective for you and your child as you seek to be the parent God has called you to be. For children who are active and boisterous, time-out takes away what they most cherish. For others who love solitude and mind play, time-out isn't a restriction at all. For some a verbal correction will crush their spirits; for others you can scream until you're blue-faced and they won't hear you until you take away that favorite toy.

It is up to you to know what brings your child joy and what brings your child pause to reflect and change. It is up to you to be consistent and to do your part to teach that child right from wrong. God will bless your efforts. Just remember: Disciplining a child has as much to do with the discipline of the parent as anything else.

some say it works) and so can bruise a spirit as well as a body. Also, physical punishment can be too easily used as a shortcut to deal with the problem quickly so the parent can get back to "real life" rather than using the discipline as a time to discuss the offense and train the child.

Whether you are reading a pro-spanking expert or an anti-spanking expert, both camps usually agree that by around the age of ten physical punishment should give way to privilege restrictions.

What is time-out about?

Time-out is really about the alternative to physical punishment: restriction of privileges. When a child misbehaves he goes to sit in whatever "time-out" place the parents have designated. This, in effect, takes away all of his privileges except creative imagination. Usually time-out chairs or places are away from the activity of the room and even out of sight of the activity of the room.

There are several wonderful benefits to using a time-out place as a form of discipline. It's really a shortened form of the old "go to your room!" but in this case the child's room doesn't become a place of punishment. If a chair is used for time-out, then that chair can be used *only* for time-out. Not so with a child's room.

The space and time to breathe is also a wonderful element to time-out. This benefits the parent as well as the child. In today's hurry-up pace a lot of behavior has to do with how fast we are running through life. Time-out gives the opportunity for reflection.

Time-out also gives the parent a consistent reaction to default to. They don't have to constantly confront the child with physical punishment or even with verbal punishment. There is a neutral zone that restricts the child without force from the parent.

That's not to say, though, that time-out works without parental input. Just as with any other form of discipline, parents need to talk with kids to make sure they understand why they were disturbed from their play and why they were restricted. Any kind of punishment without debriefing the child is mere control rather than guidance and discipline.

DISCIPLINING YOUNGER KIDS

Don't play the logic game before they can reason.

Yes, to you it makes perfect sense that we aren't getting the candy at the store because we have the same candy at home. Yes, to you it makes perfect sense that it's worth the drive to see Grandma. Yes, to you it makes perfect sense that while your neighbor's child shouldn't have taken your child's toy it is better to give than to receive anyway.

The problem is not the logic. The problem is not the common sense of it. The problem is your child doesn't yet have your sensibilities. Chances are, your child has yet to grow out of his childish worldview where now is eternal and everything revolves around his needs.

When disciplining your young child the reasons are not always the most important thing. This is why your life will be easier if your child learns early that your "no" is a definite "no" and your word is definitely trustworthy. Then as your child grows you can explain why you make the decisions you make and that you always have his best interests in mind (and after your child is over his teenage years maybe he'll believe it again).

Don't try to take the kid out of the kid.

Discipline is not the process of removing the "kid" out of your son or daughter. Life will do that quickly enough. Discipline is the process of helping her learn to control herself when the kid in her wants to be inappropriate. Of course the whole process should lead to a mature adult, but you've probably figured out by now that while you are a significant contributor to the process, you don't have complete control over the outcome.

The Bible teaches that "foolishness is bound in the heart of the child" (Proverbs 22:15) but foolishness and childishness aren't necessarily the same thing. Most children giggle more often than adults. Most children have a much harder time trying to stop giggling than adults do. When most children are exhausted they fall apart more quickly and more intensely than even adults do.

Don't try and discipline the childishness out of your child: the energy, the spirit, the wonder at the world. Try to discipline the foolishness out of your child: the willful disobedience, the dangerous carelessness, the lack of healthy boundaries. Knowing the difference is a key part of parenting.

Keep This in Mind

What is the difference between a mistake and a rebellion?

What is the difference between childishness and willful disobedience?

What is the difference between an angry, irritated parent and a parent that cares enough to discipline his or her child?

Motivation is a key to it all.

DON'T FORGET

Educate yourself.

But how do I know when my child needs correction and when she needs guidance? How do I know when it's OK to laugh at her antics and when I should reprove them?

The answer is what you're doing right now. Read what you can about kids. Read about their developmental levels and how they behave at certain ages. There are more books out there, more classes and videos and seminars than you can possibly attend. Pick a few and put yourself through an independent study. Don't have time to? Do you have time *not* to? Ask your pediatrician for some suggestions. Ask a bookstore manager what child-rearing books sell the best. Put a little effort into understanding the natural stages that a kid goes through so that you can work with him through the stage instead of wondering why your kid changes personalities every six months or less.

DISCIPLINING OLDER KIDS

It's not all about pleasing you.

Remember the days when your preschooler lived just to be with you? Remember when he got joy out of pleasing you? As your children grow and gain new interests and friends, pleasing you sure seems to slip down their priority list.

That highlights the danger of disciplining out of anger. As a young child, "keeping Mommy or Daddy from getting mad" might be enough reason to make better choices. As an older child and (can we mention it yet?) preadolescent, the desire to keep Mom and Dad happy receives competition from "fitting in with friends" and plain old "getting away with it."

Make sure your children know that the guidelines and restrictions that you place on their behavior are not all about pleasing you. They are about pleasing God and functioning in society and, yes, you are the person to decide that, no matter how coldhearted it might seem to them at any given time.

Don't try to take all the independence out of the kid.

As awkward and uncomfortable as it might feel at times, you really do want your children to have a sense of independence from you. As they grow and learn, you need to grow and learn to not be unsettled when they want to make decisions separately from you. In the same way, as you discipline, pray for discernment between what is disobedience and disrespect and what is just plain independence.

Your children's independence can be disconcerting for several reasons. One is your own protectiveness for your children. If they feel they can make too many decisions on their own they might hurt themselves. If they get too far out of your grasp, you might not be able to pull them in when they make a mistake. This is the kind of tightrope that will not go away anytime soon. Another reason is your protectiveness for yourself and your belongings and your family. Who wants to be embarrassed by a child in trouble? Who wants to have possessions damaged by a child who wasn't careful when no one was looking?

As you continue to work with your children through their school-age years, be proactive about helping them realize their independence. Find areas where you can offer them decision-making opportunities in which a

The Power Struggle

CATCH A CLUE

Life is filled with power struggles. When you haggle at the flea market there's a power struggle. When you climb the corporate ladder there's a power struggle. In that sense, parenting isn't a lot different. Here are two or more people vying for control and independence at the same time. You need to know that your children will obey you. You need to know this for their safety and for their path to maturity. Your children need to know that they won't always be controlled by you. They live in the hope that they will one day manage their own lives and make their own decisions.

Power struggles are a *part* of raising kids. The challenge before you is to not let your relationship with your child become all about power. If every interaction is becoming a power struggle, stop and evaluate. Look aggressively for ways to interact over noncompetitive issues.

You may come to a place where nothing you say is good enough for your child. But even at its worst, don't let your own ego get wrapped up in the relationship. Find ways to agree with your children's positions, to value their opinions as long as, in the end, they live within your ground rules.

poor choice will not devastate either one of you. They will find decision-making opportunities whether you help or not. Try to stay a step ahead and minimize the potential damage.

Partner with them in their plight to be free from you and you'll have a better chance of having them with you a lot longer.

Do some hanging out.

Whatever you do, don't let your interactions dissolve down to the point where you only interact in disciplinary situations. Yes, everyone is busy. Perhaps there are other children in the home. Yes, as they get older they get involved in more and more activities. Yes, if *you* don't make sure that there is some time to hang out and stay connected no one will.

As with any relationship, discipline is more effective if there is a solid relationship with some trust preceding it. That is even more important as children age and have access to more relationships and influences. It's too easy to become the person who steps in only when something's wrong. You can be sure that if you become that person your discipline will not be as effective—if it's effective at all.

Think of it this way. What if you saw a parent only interact with her preschooler to punish or correct him? You'd call it neglect. It's the same thing when your older child only hears from you when you have something negative to discuss.

(OMMUNI(ATION, (OMMUNI(ATION, (OMMUNI(ATION

Communicating with your spouse communicates to the kids

How you communicate with your children is important to the effectiveness of your discipline. But just as important is how you communicate with your spouse in the presence of your children. Here are some tips to remember:

- When your child asks for permission and you are unsure, remember to ask him if he has asked your spouse.
- When your child asks you for permission in the presence of your spouse, take time to ask for confirmation from your spouse.
- Don't vent your marriage frustrations to your kids or in the presence of your kids.
- Treat your spouse with respect and, even if you are angry, neutrality in the presence of your kids.
- Talk with your spouse about discipline and about why you each make the decisions that you do in regards to the children.

Communicating with your child

You communicate with your child in a thousand ways. You've taught your child some of the most important lessons that you will ever teach her before she has even gained her verbal skills. You communicate with your child by the way you look at her, the kind of attention you give her, by how quickly you respond when she calls your name, by the way you listen when she has something to say. You communicate nonverbally with your child a thousand times for every word you say to her. Here are some tips for communicating with your children nonverbally:

- Make a point to look them in the eyes when you greet them to get a sense of their well-being.
- Touch them occasionally as you listen and as you talk.
- When they approach you make it a point (when possible) to release what is in your hands and turn toward them.

Here are some tips for communicating with your children verbally:

- When you are having a hard time concentrating on what they are saying, make a practice to summarize it back to them ("Let me see if I'm understanding you, you're saying…").
- Tell them that you like them (as well as love them) and what you like.

Don't Let This Happen to You

CATCH A CLUE

When parents say…	Kids hear…
Maybe.	If we keep asking it'll happen.
Don't make me say that again.	We've got a few more minutes before they get serious.
I'm headed up the stairs!	They're just about serious.
I… 2…	We'd better do it now!
I'm busy right now.	Now is a good time to get away with something.
No.	This is going to be harder than I thought.

- Be willing to discuss why you make the decisions you do, even if you aren't willing to discuss it in the heat of the moment.
- Watch your tone of voice. Think about your tone when you talk to someone you respect and revere. Use that tone sometimes with your kids. Use a respectful tone all the time.

Communicating after an offense, in the tense times

One of the key times to communicate with your child is after you've had to discipline him. You remember how it is to be a punished kid. The guilt mingles with everything else inside of you and there is that part of you that wonders if the relationship is going to be OK. There is a fine art to communicating to your child that the relationship is not broken, but that he is not out of the doghouse. *Say it!* Even if the best you can drum up is a distant, neutral tone, say to him that you are not at all happy with his actions, but that you value him and you will both work this through. Let him know that this tension is not a permanent state.

READY TO MOVE ON?

So far, this book has covered some basic principals that parents can apply no matter the age of their children. Now, let's focus a little and get age specific. . .

SECTION 7
INFANTS

. . .AND ONE ON THE WAY

THE PREGNANCY

Congratulations, you're going to be a parent! For the next several months you'll have a front-row seat for the miracle of life. While your unborn child grows and develops in the safety of the womb, there are things you can do to make life easier for you, your family, and your baby.

Find a doctor you're comfortable with.
Arm yourself with a list of questions and the names of several obstetricians in your area (or at least the names of those covered by your medical insurance). Find the one who best suits your needs. If you have strong feelings about certain elements of childbirth—let's say you oppose the use of forceps during delivery, for example—look for a doctor who will accommodate your preferences. Beyond finding someone who shares your beliefs, though, you will need to find a doctor who puts you at ease. If this is your first child, you will likely have dozens of questions for your obstetrician. It is vitally important that you feel comfortable enough with him or her to ask those questions.

Don't try to bear the burden alone.
Pregnancy can be a long and lonely experience—if you allow it to be. That's why it's important that you surround yourself with people who genuinely care about you and your child, as well as people who have

experienced pregnancy and childbirth. Ideally, the first place you would look for support is from your spouse. Remember, though, a man can only imagine what it's like to carry a baby around for forty weeks. He can sympathize, but he can't empathize. Anything you can do to help him understand how you're feeling will benefit both of you. Help your spouse recognize your needs, both physical and emotional, during (and after) your pregnancy.

In addition to your spouse, you should also try to find some experts to help you throughout your pregnancy. How many of your good friends have given birth? How many of your close relatives are mothers? Don't be shy about asking for their advice and encouragement. After all, only a fellow mother really understands what you're facing. If you have trustworthy people around you who can tell you whether the things you're experiencing are normal or not, you will greatly increase your happiness and comfort during your pregnancy.

Remember that your health affects your baby's health.
While it may be impossible to guarantee that your baby will be healthy, there are several steps you can take to improve the little one's chances. The first thing you need to do is eliminate all alcohol and tobacco products. (Do we really need to tell you that this also includes marijuana, cocaine, and all other illegal drugs?) It's not a matter of cutting back; it's a matter of quitting altogether. If you're a longtime smoker or drinker, take whatever steps are necessary to quit. Do it now. It's not just your health that you're jeopardizing anymore—it's your baby's.

Talk to your doctor about your diet. Find out what foods you should and shouldn't be eating. You'll probably discover that most things are okay in moderation, but it's always best to find out for sure.

Explore your options.
The concept of a "traditional" childbirth is rapidly becoming obsolete. With

so many options to choose from, there's really no such thing as a *standard* procedure anymore. If you'd prefer to give birth in a sitting position, it can be arranged. If you'd like to have your baby at home, you can. If you'd like your child to be born underwater, you can find professionals to deliver your baby aquatically. If you believe the pain of childbirth is an integral part of the delivery, you can refuse anesthetic. If pain holds no appeal for you, you can opt for an epidural or a spinal block. The point is, there is a world of options at your fingertips. You can choose the way you want your child to come into the world.

If you're like most expectant parents, you'll find that approximately one out of every twenty stories you hear has relevance to you. Of course, that won't keep you from worrying and wondering about the other nineteen.

It would be naive to suggest that you not allow other people's stories to affect you. But there *are* a few things you can do to lessen their impact. The next time you find yourself cornered by a mother intent on sharing the gory details of her pregnancy, labor, or delivery, remind yourself of three things:

CATCH A CLUE

Free Advice Available

A curious thing happens when you're pregnant. Complete strangers—people who otherwise wouldn't give you a second look on the street—suddenly feel compelled to share the most personal details of their own pregnancies with you.

1. Every pregnancy is unique. One person's experiences have absolutely no bearing on another person's experiences.
2. For every complication, there are hundreds of things that go right during a pregnancy. The odds are with you.
3. Sometimes people—well, *embellish* their stories for maximum effect. In other words, don't believe everything you hear.

INCOMING!

PREPARING FOR THE NEWBORN

Ready or not, you've got a baby on the way. In a matter of months, your life will never be the same again. Get a jump on the craziness that lies ahead by preparing your house, your car, and your family for what is to come.

PREPARING YOUR HOUSE

With a newborn on the way, childproofing your home may not be at the top of your priority list right now. That's understandable. But don't delay the inevitable too long. Mobility (and all of the dangers it presents) is just around the corner. In fact, your baby will probably be able to locate a hazard or two in your home long before he learns to crawl or walk. While it may be impossible to anticipate everything that might pose a danger to your child, you can get a good start on making your home baby-friendly by following these tips:

- Make sure your child will be sleeping safely. Most new cribs are designed to meet strict safety standards. If you're using a hand-me-down crib, though, you'll need to make sure that it's safe. The slats of the crib should be no more than 2–3/8" apart. Any wider than that, and your baby's body could squeeze through them. The mattress should be the same size as the crib, with no gaps. Make sure that all screws, bolts, and other pieces are tightly in place. Check to see that none of the corner posts are over 1/16 of an inch above the end panels. If they are, your baby's clothing could catch on them, causing your child to strangle. Finally, always keep the rails up when your baby's in the crib. Don't just check the crib in your baby's nursery. Check all of the cribs that he may sleep in—the one at the baby-sitter's house, the one at Grandma's house, the one in the church nursery, and so on.

- Make a habit of picking up buttons, paper clips, coins, safety pins, and anything else on the floor that your child may be tempted to put in his mouth.

- Take a tour of your house at your baby's eye level. Crawl around on your hands and knees, looking for potential hazards and unsafe places. You may be surprised at what you find. Install outlet plates and plug protectors on electrical outlets throughout your home. Keep electrical cords secured with lamp and appliance cord keepers. Block all stairways with safety gates that fit snugly. Install flexible doorstops to keep your baby's fingers from being pinched.

- Anchor all bookcases, entertainment centers, dressers, and other heavy pieces of furniture to the wall. Once your baby learns to pull himself up, he is potentially able to pull unanchored pieces of furniture down on top of himself.

- Store all cleaning products, insecticides, and medicines in their original containers and in places where your child can't get to them. Use drawer latches and doorknob covers to keep certain items off limits to your child.

- Stock your medicine cabinet with essential items. Depending on the age of your child, these items might include the following: diphenhydramine hydrochloride (to ease allergy symptoms), ibuprofen and acetaminophen (to be used only with doctor's permission), some kind of calibrated measuring tool, saline nose drops and nasal bulb syringe (to unclog stuffy noses), thermometer (preferably a rectal mercury or digital model), rubbing alcohol, age-appropriate nail clippers, colloidal oatmeal (to ease the itching of rashes and insect bites), sunscreen (SPF 15 or higher), petroleum jelly, diaper rash ointment, emetrol (to relieve nausea in a child over two years old), oral electrolyte solution (to rehydrate a child with diarrhea or vomiting), cotton swabs, tweezers, and syrup of ipecac (to be used only under the instructions of a poison control center).

PREPARING YOUR CAR

Car seats are no longer just a good idea for babies; they are the law. Make sure that when you pick up your new bundle of joy from the hospital, the car seat he rides home in is as safe as possible.

When you install the seat, follow the manufacturer's instructions carefully. (While you're at it, send in the registration card that comes with the seat so that you will be notified if and when the seat is recalled.) Make sure that the seat you've chosen fits well in your vehicle. Tighten the safety belt so that the seat doesn't move from side to side or toward the front of the car. When you put your child in the seat, make sure that the shoulder straps fit snugly (but not too tightly) across his body.

If your vehicle has a passenger-side air bag, you *must* put the car seat in the backseat. Until your child celebrates his first birthday and weighs more than twenty pounds, he must face backwards when riding in the car.

PREPARING YOUR CHILD'S SIBLINGS

Few things are as disruptive to a child's life as the arrival of a baby brother or sister. Here are some suggestions that may help your child understand the changes that are on the way. Choose the ideas that you think will work best for your young one.

- Read books about new babies and encourage your child to talk about what he thinks new babies are like and what changes he thinks will occur within your home. (Be warned, though. Often such discussions lead to the inevitable question, "Where do babies come from?")
- Go through your child's baby book with him, showing him how you cared for him as a baby.
- If possible, bring home a friend's baby for a day to show your child how babies are cared for.
- If you're planning a bed or room change for your child, do it before the baby arrives so that your child doesn't feel put out by the baby.
- As much as possible, include your child in the household preparations for the new baby.
- If he's old enough, let your child go with you to the doctor. If possible, let him listen to the baby's heartbeat or perhaps even see an ultrasound image.
- Buy a book on fetal development so that you and your child can trace the growth of the baby.
- Prepare for your stay in the hospital by recording bedtime stories on cassette tapes that can be played while you're gone. Say "good night" to your child at the end of each tape.
- Buy your child a T-shirt that says, "I'm going to be a big brother (or sister)!"
- Enroll your child in a sibling preparation class. (Yes, some hospitals and other organizations actually offer sibling preparation classes.)

"WELCOME HOME, BABY!"

How do you picture your first few weeks of parenthood? How much of an adjustment do you think it will be to have a new baby in the house? How much will your everyday routines change? It would be an interesting exercise to jot down your thoughts and expectations in a journal, put it away for a while, and then retrieve it and read what you wrote. Chances are, you'll marvel at how naive and utterly unprepared you were for the changes that lay ahead. Here are just a few of the ways your life may change in the next few months.

DISRUPTED SCHEDULES

"You don't know what you've got 'til it's gone." That's what you'll be saying about your free time once your child arrives. Gone are the days when you could call up a friend for an impromptu lunch date. With a new baby to care for, even the most mundane tasks—things like shopping for groceries and working out at the health club—require the planning and precision of a Space Shuttle launch. Who's going to care for the baby while you're gone? When is the next scheduled feeding? How long can you go before you have to pump? These are just a few of the questions you'll have to answer every time you walk out the door.

If you're used to coming and going as you please or if you cherish spontaneity, you're in for a challenge. Like it or not, your way of living has been altered. You're now operating on Baby Time! In time, you'll find a middle ground between your scheduling needs and your baby's. Until you do, your best bet is to learn how to get things done on Baby Time.

FREQUENT EXHAUSTION

The most practical piece of advice any new parent can get may be summed up in five words: *Nap when your baby does.* Not long after you return home from the hospital, you'll discover just how precious a commodity sleep is. That adorable, harmless-looking bundle of joy you bring home with you will deprive you of rest more thoroughly than a five-man jackhammer crew working double shifts outside your bedroom window. It won't be long before you hear yourself saying things like, "We were able to sleep in until 4:00 this morning!" or

WOW!

One Father's Experience

"When my daughter was born, I was overwhelmed by the joy that most new parents probably feel. Later, though, I experienced some emotions that took me by surprise. When I laid my daughter in her bassinet for the first time, I was overcome by a feeling of sadness. It was heartbreaking for me to see someone so fragile and helpless, someone so totally dependent on other people for her survival.

"To tell you the truth, I was also a little scared. It hit me that I was one of the two people this baby was depending on. As much as I hate to admit it, I'm not perfect. In fact, I'm decidedly imperfect. I make quite a few mistakes every day. How could I be expected to fulfill another human being's most vital needs?

"What I discovered, though, is that the Lord equipped me—just as I believe He equips all parents—with caretaking resources I never knew I had. I was surprised at how quickly I was able to hone the skills I needed to assist my wife in caring for our daughter. That's not to say that I've become a role model for fathers everywhere. My family can tell you that I still make quite a few mistakes every day. But as I see my daughter develop and grow, I can tell you that I'm proud of the job my wife and I have done so far."
—**Randy, Mount Prospect, Illinois**

"Amy went three hours between feedings last night!"

It doesn't take a trained observer to spot new parents. All you have to do is look for the telltale bags under the eyes and the "zombie shuffle" in their walk. Catch them early enough in their parenting experience and you may even see them nod off in midconversation. Being a parent is an exhausting responsibility.

The best way to avoid demonstrating the physical traits of a new parent is to learn to sleep when your baby does. Of course, there will be a million other things you'll need to do when the little one finally dozes off, but take our word for it: None of them is more important than recharging your physical batteries with a brief nap.

SUDDEN INSECURITY

As a new parent, you may find yourself struggling with insecurity and guilt. Regardless of how naturally confident you are or how much you tell yourself that no one knows your child like you do, occasionally (or frequently) you'll find yourself questioning your parenting choices. You'll wrestle with decisions you've made, doubting your judgment. You'll start to feel guilty about the things you've done, or haven't done, for your child. In especially difficult moments, you might even convince yourself that every parent in the world knows what they're doing, except you.

It would be easy to say, "Don't let those feelings get you down." But that wouldn't be very helpful, would it? Instead, we'll suggest that you keep the lines of heavenly communication open. Pray about your decisions, big and small. Ask the Lord to guide your parenting choices. Trust in His judgment, rather than your own.

THE BABY INVENTORY

CHECKLISTS FOR NEW PARENTS

One of the toughest tasks facing new parents is figuring out exactly what their newborn is going to need. Before you begin any baby shopping excursion, consult the following list of the essentials. Next to each item, you'll find the recommended number to buy, as well as a comment or two to consider.

For the Bedroom Closet

Obviously, your baby's clothing needs will depend on the time of year he's born. The following list is simply a general guideline of what to look for. The number of items needed will change on a seasonal basis.

- **Diapers (60 per week).** Obviously you're going to have to choose between cloth and disposable diapers. Both kinds have their strengths and weaknesses. Whichever style you choose, though, you'll need plenty of them.
- **Undershirts (5).** The pullover style with snaps at the bottom are easy to put on and remove. What's more, they'll keep your baby's belly covered.
- **Nightgowns (5).** Most new products are designed to meet rigid safety standards. If you use hand-me-downs, though, you'll need to make sure that all sleepwear is flame resistant.
- **Blanket sleepers (2).** The bag type will work well until your child learns to pull himself up.

- **Diaper cover (1).** This is for aesthetic purposes only, for mothers and their dress-wearing daughters who prefer diapers to be hidden.
- **Socks (2 pairs).** For your own sanity, find socks that can't be kicked off easily. You'll be amazed at how quickly your baby will learn to shed his socks.
- **Stretchies (3).** For the uninitiated, stretchies are outfits with feet in them.
- **Rompers (3).** Likewise, rompers are short-sleeved, one-piece outfits that snap at the crotch.
- **Bibs (2).** It's never too early to begin protecting your child's clothing from spitups and other messy mishaps.
- **Sweaters (2).** Babies need warmth even in the summer months.
- **Hats (2).** You'll need a lightweight lid to keep the sun off your baby's head in the summer and a heavier model (preferably with earflaps) to keep the warmth in during the winter.
- **Snowsuit (1).** The bag style with attached mittens generally provide the most warmth.

For the Linen Closet
- **Receiving blankets (6).** It's a good idea to keep your baby wrapped up snugly during his first few weeks out of the womb. Keep one or two blankets in your baby's stroller in case you need them while you're out.
- **Square cloth diapers (12).** Even if you're using disposable diapers, it's a good idea to have some of these all-purpose items around to protect your clothes and your furniture from your baby's spitup.
- **Terry-cloth towels (3).** Go for the hooded variety. Not only will your child look cute in them, his head will be kept warm after bath time.
- **Washcloths (3).** Softer is better when it comes to bath-time fabrics.

For the Crib
- **Fitted sheets (3).** Keep in mind that the more snugly the sheets fit the mattress, the safer your baby is.
- **Quilted mattress pads (2).** You could probably get away without buying these, if you had to. They do provide extra comfort for your baby, though.
- **Waterproof pads (4).** These protect the crib and other furniture items from the various bodily liquids produced by babies.
- **Bassinet blankets (2).** Make sure they're washable and that they don't have long fringe or loose threads on them.

For the Changing Table
- **Baby soap.** Don't overuse soap during bath time. It has a tendency to dry out babies' skin.
- **Baby shampoo.** The no-tears variety is strongly recommended. Nothing ruins an enjoyable bath time faster than stinging eyes.
- **Baby oil.** For skin as smooth as a baby's. . .well, you know.
- **Cornstarch.** This cooking ingredient can also be used to dry areas of a baby's skin that a towel can't get to—most notably, under the baby's chin.
- **Diaper rash ointment.** With so many different brands available, your best bet is to get your doctor's recommendation.
- **Petroleum jelly.** Not only is it the ideal lubricant for such unpleasant tasks as anal temperature-taking, it's also a great moisturizer for your baby's skin.
- **Diaper wipes.** These handy items are a diaper-changer's dream. Just make sure that your baby isn't allergic to them.
- **Cotton balls.** These are the best things to use when cleaning your baby's eyes and umbilical cord residue.
- **Baby nail clippers.** Left unchecked, your baby's fingernails and toenails can become dangerously long and sharp in a relatively short time.

- **Baby hairbrush and comb.** Even babies want to look their best.
- **Nasal aspirator.** This bulb syringe is used to unclog stuffed noses.
- **Thermometer.** Unfortunately for everyone involved, most experts recommend rectal thermometers.

For the Kitchen
- **Bottles with nipples.** If you're bottle-feeding, you'll need four 4-ounce bottles and twelve 8-ounce bottles. If you're supplementing your breast feeding with a bottle, you'll only need two of each size. It's always a good idea, though, to have an extra bottle around somewhere for emergencies.
- **Baby formula utensils.** If you're bottle-feeding or even if you're supplementing, you'll need to be able to measure out precise quantities of water and formula.
- **Sterilizer.** You don't want your little bundle of joy getting sick because of unsanitary bottles or nipples, do you?

For the Bedroom
- **Crib.** The bars of your baby's crib should be no further apart than two and three-eighths inches. Make sure that there are no splinters or cracks in the wood that your baby can find.
- **Crib mattress.** Firmness is probably the most important feature of a crib mattress. Look for one that will support your baby.
- **Bumpers.** Make sure that they fit snugly around the crib.

For the Bathroom
- **Baby tub.** Among the features you'll want to look for are easy portability, quick drainage, roominess, and convenient washability. Beyond that, look for something with bright, colorful pictures on it for your child to enjoy every bath time.

For the World Outside

- **Car seat.** Many new car seats double as baby carriers and can be quickly detached from a base that stays belted in the car.
- **Stroller.** Look for a mobile baby unit that includes an adjustable reclining seat, large wheels, good brakes, and easy foldability.
- **Diaper bag.** Look for a bag with several different compartments (preferably one of which is waterproof).

WHAT TO EXPECT

DEVELOPMENTAL MILESTONES FOR THE FIRST YEAR OF YOUR CHILD'S LIFE

When do children usually learn their first word? At what age do they go from drinking from a bottle to drinking from a cup? This developmental outline will give you a general idea of what the near future holds for your newborn.

It's important to emphasize, though, that these time frames are approximate. Every child is unique and progresses at a unique pace. If your child isn't able to roll from her stomach to her back by the time she's two months old, don't panic. Chances are, she's ahead of schedule in another area of development.

One Month
- Your one-month-old may be able to raise his head slightly while he's lying on his stomach.
- He may be able to focus on your face.
- He may also be able to respond to a noise, either by crying or by growing quiet.
- He will sleep about fourteen-and-a-half hours a day, with an eight-and-a-half-hour stretch at night and three two-hour naps during the day.
- He will eat every two to five hours and will gain about two pounds if he's bottle-fed and one-and-a-half pounds if he's breast-fed.

Two Months
- Your two-month-old may be able to hold his head up while he's lying on his stomach.
- He may be able to smile at you.
- He may also be able to follow with his eyes an object held about six inches in front of his face.

Three Months
- Your three-month-old may be able to get your attention by cooing and gurgling.
- He may be able to laugh or squeal in delight.
- He will sleep about fourteen-and-a-half hours a day, with a ten-hour stretch at night and three one-and-a-half-hour naps during the day.

Four Months
- Your four-month-old may be able to focus intently on an object or person and follow it with his eyes in all directions.
- He may be able to hold his head steady when he's upright.
- He may also be able to grab a rattle that is held out to him.

Five Months
- Your five-month-old may be able to recognize familiar sounds or voices.
- He may be able to entertain himself by playing with his hands or fingers.
- He may also be able to roll over from stomach to back.

Six Months
- Your six-month-old may be able to sit without being supported.
- He may be able to eat strained foods.
- He may get his first tooth.
- He may also be able to roll over from back to stomach.
- He will sleep about fourteen-and-a-half hours a day, with a twelve-hour stretch at night and two one-hour naps during the day.

Seven Months
- Your seven-month-old may be able to feed himself a cracker.
- He may be able to make a "raspberry" sound.
- He may also be able to work to get a toy that is out of reach.

Eight Months
- Your eight-month-old may be able to play peekaboo with you.
- He may be able to bear some weight on his legs while you're holding him upright.
- He may be able to recognize strangers.
- He may also be able to pass a toy from one hand to the other.

Nine Months
- Your nine-month-old may be able to look around for an object that has fallen on the floor.
- He may be able to get into a sitting position from his stomach.
- He may also be able to say "Dada" or "Mama" at will.
- He will sleep about fourteen and a half hours a day, with an eleven-hour stretch at night and two one-and-a-half-hour naps during the day.

Ten Months
- Your ten-month-old may be able to stand while holding on to something.
- He may be able to pull up to a standing position from sitting.
- He may also be able to crawl.
- He may also be able to put up a fight if you try to take a toy away.

Eleven Months
- Your eleven-month-old may be able to pick up tiny objects with his thumb and forefinger.
- He may be able to understand the word "No."
- He may also be able to wave bye-bye.

Twelve Months

- Your twelve-month-old may be able to walk while holding on to furniture.
- He may be able to play patty-cake.
- He may also be able to drink from a cup by himself.

SECTION 8

TODDLER

FROM CREEPY CRAWLY TO TODDLER

So your crawler is now a walker! Just when you thought you had completely childproofed your house, new dangers suddenly appear. The dining room table is the same height as your toddler, but no one notices until she bumps her head. The family dog is no longer unreachable in its favorite chair. Your toddler may even be able to reach items on low tables. She follows you so closely you are afraid to turn around for fear of knocking her over.

But take heart. With the advent of walking comes a new independence for you and your toddler. You don't have to carry her everywhere since she is free to move about and explore her world just like everyone else. Your toddler has no desire to be confined—in a car seat, a play yard, your arms—for any length of time. There is so much to see, taste, smell, and touch, and every toddler deserves the opportunity to learn—with your careful supervision.

FRIENDS, ENTERTAINMENT, AND TOYS

At this stage, you have complete control over your child's choice of friends. Friends from church or former coworkers who have children close to your toddler's age may be willing to make weekly "play dates."

A "play date" is a special time set aside for you and your toddler to join other parents with toddlers in someone's home in order to allow the children to socialize. During these gatherings children learn how to interact with others and how to communicate with people other than their parents. Until about the age of three, your toddler will play *next to* another child rather than play *with* another child. Sharing is a concept understood in later toddler years, beginning around two-and-a-half to three years of age, so don't expect your young toddler to understand how to share with others until that time.

One of the major benefits of the play date is that parents are also present. Finally, a chance for you to get out of the house and speak to adults! What better place for you to share your concerns about your child or discuss different methods of discipline. Maybe you'll even share that funny story about your toddler's recent experimentation with crayons on the living room wall. Maybe you'll make a point to discuss everything but children.

CATCH A CLUE

Five Easy Activities For Toddlers

1. Cut different shapes from construction paper and play matching games.
2. Stack blocks and count as you stack. See how many blocks can be stacked before the tower falls.
3. "Paint" the sidewalk or driveway with water using a plastic bowl of water and an old paintbrush. Take note how quickly the pictures disappear on sunny days.
4. Draw with a roll of paper, sketch pad, or extra computer paper and a box of crayons. Be sure to save some of those early drawings!
5. Roll a ball back and forth on the floor, or "bowl" with a ball and three empty 2-liter soda pop bottles.

THE INFLUENCE OF LITTLE FRIENDS

Whenever your toddler interacts with others—whether in the church nursery, at a play date or preschool—he or she will pick up others' actions and attitudes. When those actions and attitudes are improper, you will need to discuss that with your child. Remember your toddler is just that—a toddler. She will mimic what she sees. He will repeat what he hears. Your toddler doesn't know if a specific word is bad or good unless you tell her so. Therefore, she won't understand if your reaction to that word is particularly harsh. Simply take your toddler aside and explain to her that Mommy and Daddy don't say that word and why. Then remind her that she shouldn't say it either. Your toddler understands quite a bit and will respond better to reason than harsh reaction.

A major concern of most parents is how to entertain their toddler. You know by now that babies need constant attention—well, now your baby is walking! He doesn't just cry when he wants something. . .he cries, walks over, and pulls on your pant leg and won't leave you alone until you DO something.

What now? Books? Videos? Games? Every child is different and each responds in his or her own way to every form of entertainment. Books are one of the best forms of entertainment your money can buy. Have your toddler sit on your lap as you read. Point out and name the pictures and colors on each page and you'll be surprised at how quickly he will be able to repeat what you say with accuracy. Let him turn the pages—books with thick pages, "board books," work best with younger toddlers—give each character a different voice and read until your throat is dry! There is no substitute for Mommy or Daddy giving undivided attention in the form of reading a book.

So what happens when you are too tired to read, your throat hurts, the checkbook must be balanced, and the little one is in serious need of something to do? There are thousands of videos and children's television programs tailored to entertain each level of toddlerhood. Cartoons, puppets, interesting shapes dancing across the screen to classical music, other children singing—something will capture and hold your toddler's attention.

VIDEOS

But a few words of caution regarding videos. ALWAYS watch the video yourself, either with your toddler or before your toddler sees it. Some cartoons can be frightening to a small child while other shows may spout political or religious views you don't agree with (it really does happen!). Some may instill fears or bring about bad attitudes. You will not be able to control everything your child sees and hears, but for now you can control what your toddler watches on the TV.

THE BOTTOM LINE

Health and Safety

There are entire books dedicated to this very subject, giving information regarding first aid, infant and toddler CPR, childhood diseases, home remedies, etc. We recommend *The Complete Book of Baby and Child Care* by **Grace Ketterman, M.D.**, a good book for parents.

GAMES

Another excellent form of entertainment for toddlers is games you can play with them. We're not talking about the $30 games from the toy store, rather, we're talking about the old standbys such as "Hide and Seek," "I Spy," and many others. And always remember that your toddler is not as quick or smart as you. Don't get frustrated when she hides behind a standing lamp or under a blanket in the middle of the room. As she gets older she'll find better places to hide. Likewise, don't hide too well from your toddler—you may have to keep calling her name so she can easily find you.

"I Spy" is a learning game for toddlers who are just getting a handle on colors, shapes, etc. You start by saying, "I spy with my little eye something blue," or any other color you choose. The first thing your child names with that color is the right answer. As your toddler gets older, the game develops more specifics, "I spy with my little eye something bumpy." And your toddler will begin to play back by giving you the clue.

Toy stores make billions of dollars each year selling toys that promise to entertain your child for hours on end! From experience we can tell you that a toddler's attention span with a toy is approximately fifteen to twenty minutes, then they move on to something else. So before you spend, see what is around your home that might interest your little one: a cardboard box, a plastic bowl and spoon, pots and pans (if you don't mind loud noises), stackable plastic cups, a box of plastic curlers, the list goes on and on. Basically, if it is safe for your child to play with—nothing that can choke, strangle, pinch, or cut—then let your toddler have fun.

If you plan to buy any toy for your toddler, be sure it is age appropriate. The packaging of the toy will include an area which states, "For ages 3 and older," or something similar. This is done to inform parents of what toy is safe for your age toddler. Toddler-appropriate toys typically contain no small parts (choking hazard), no long cords or strings (strangling hazard), or sharp edges.

OUTDOORS

Outdoor play is a little more tricky. You have much more control over the indoor play environment of your child than the outdoors with its sticks, pebbles, bugs, grass, and so many other things your little one will attempt to taste. Outdoor play allows for messier activities. Toddlers love playing with water in plastic cups or bowls, sidewalk chalk, balls, sand, a pile of leaves, snow. . .remember kids and their clothes are washable! Always keep an eye on your little one when outside, the main reason being that you don't want to lose him or her due to accident, wandering away, or abduction. Also, toddlers tend to put everything in their mouths. You'll want to get the pebbles or dandelions out of your sweetie's hand before she swallows them!

You and your toddler will benefit if you allow yourself to become a child now and then. Don't be afraid to roll in the grass or play in the sprinkler. Draw sidewalk chalk pictures and get down and dirty in the sandbox. You and your clothes are washable too, so don't let this period of your child's life pass by with you as a simple bystander.

FINDING PEACE WHILE LIVING WITH A TODDLER

Parenthood is a full-time job. And if you are a stay-at-home parent of a toddler, chances are you have a 168-hour work week, give or take a few hours. Having a toddler (or two) of your own, you probably fall asleep as you fall into bed, completely exhausted from the day's activities. You're not just a mom; you're a referee, counselor, teacher, medic, cook, and maid. When and where do you get a little peace?!?

You may find that nap time is the most peaceful time of the day. If you have more than one child, try to get them both onto the same nap schedule so you can have complete quiet for the duration of nap time. Use that time to do something relaxing—read, take a bath, chat with a friend, or just sit in the sun. Better yet, take a nap yourself! It is vitally important to do something you enjoy during this "quiet time" so you can "recharge your batteries." Chances are you can do household chores while your toddler plays at your feet, but it's difficult to concentrate on the latest best-seller when you have to put it down every thirty seconds to wipe Junior's nose.

Early morning is another quiet time a parent can enjoy. Get up before your toddler awakens. Enjoy a daily quiet time, a cup of coffee, and a hot shower. Being completely ready for the day before your toddler even crawls out of bed does wonders for your mood.

Try to get out of the house once a week, whether it is to the gym or dinner and a movie. Parents deserve a break from the monotony of household chores and speaking baby talk. Paying a sitter is well worth the retention of your sanity.

There are many ways to have peace within the home with your toddler awake and present. Have a good relationship with your spouse. A toddler who sees that Mommy and Daddy love and respect each other will feel good about himself and you. Agree on methods of discipline and rules (no running indoors, etc.). Even a toddler can figure out how to pit one parent against the other in order to get his way. Listen to your toddler and respond honestly to his questions. Encourage his interests—if he loves to put puzzles together, supply him with puzzles; if she likes to play dress-up, give her some of your old clothes. Don't harp on mistakes. Make discipline swift and the punishment fit the crime. A toddler won't make the connection between his refusal to eat dinner tonight resulting in no cartoons on Saturday morning.

Pieces of Peace

CATCH A CLUE

Toddlers don't allow parents much time to themselves during the day. Here are a few tips to make the most of those quiet moments:

1. Spend time with devotions and prayer to refresh and renew your spirit.
2. Do something you like to do (reading, gardening, exercising, etc.).
3. Enjoy a quiet conversation with your spouse or a close friend.
4. Put on the earphones and listen to your favorite music.
5. Take a long, hot, uninterrupted shower.
6. Listen to quietness and revel in silence.

Above all, remember that you will make mistakes too. Admit mistakes to your child and apologize to your toddler when you have wronged him. From this he will learn that (1) even though you make mistakes, he still loves you, and in turn (2) when he makes mistakes he'll still be loved by you.

SECTION 9
SCHOOL-AGE KIDS

PUBLIC, PRIVATE, OR HOMESCHOOL?

It used to be that, when your child was ready to begin kindergarten, you simply sent him to the local public school. The only other option may have been a parochial school, or perhaps a pricey private school. But times have changed.

As Christian parents became increasingly concerned with the downturn of many of the public schools, Christian schools began springing up all over the country—often in church basements. Curriculum began to be developed for these fledgling schools. But they had to be supported by payments from the parents—often meaning many could not afford it.

As a result, many parents opted to simply keep their children at home and teach them there—hearkening back to the pioneer days when many of the great minds of our country were taught at home. As the homeschool movement grew, curriculum was developed, conferences planned, support groups organized. Today hundreds of thousands of children stay at home every day to be "homeschooled."

So what do you do? You have a local Christian school—it'll cost you, but you're willing to make the sacrifice. You have the public school ready and waiting—your tax dollars at work. But you also know that you can simply keep your child at home and join with a network of like-minded people. What should you do? Let's consider some of the pros and cons of each kind of school situation. Ultimately, your decision will be grounded in prayer as you consider your family's situation and your child's needs. Educating yourself will help you gain a clearer picture.

THE LOCAL PUBLIC SCHOOL

For many Christian families, this is simply a matter of course. They know that their budget cannot afford the Christian school, and for one reason or another, choose not to homeschool. But are you "throwing your children to the wolves" when you send them through the doors of the public school?

Surely not. In fact, the children who will thrive best at the public

Get Involved

"My daughter received a permission slip for a 'health' field trip. The kids began to call it the 'sex' field trip (this was fifth grade!) and, of course, I began wondering what this was all about. The fifth graders would be going to a science museum that focused on the human body and would attend a session on the male and female reproductive systems. I called the museum to ask about the program. The explanation seemed innocent enough, but only one thing concerned me—the woman who taught the course never separated the boys from the girls. I had already taught my daughter the facts of life, so I decided that she didn't really need this extra training, especially not in a room full of fifth-grade boys. So we opted out of the field trip—and she didn't mind because she thought she'd be embarrassed anyway.

"One side note is interesting, however. I did not call the school regarding this trip because this was the first time they were going to go to this particular museum, so I assumed they wouldn't know anything. As it turned out, my daughter's teacher (not a Christian, but older and old-fashioned) *did* ask for the boys and girls to be separated for the class I mentioned above. If I had called and asked, I would have found support. The point is, *know* what is going on. Ask questions. Be involved. You needn't make a lot of waves—pick your battles carefully. But stand up for Christ in a place where He is desperately needed. You may find that support comes from many places—parents who are not Christians will often side with you, and other Christian parents will be glad you knew what was going on and let them know."

—Sasha, Tulsa, Oklahoma

school are the Christian children. Why? Because when questionable material is taught, or questionable situations come up, who has the moral grounding to deal with it? The Christian home. Which child has the parents who will explain that people are not evolved from amoebas? The Christian child. Which child has the moral fiber to stand up for what is right? The Christian child, because he or she has been grounded in the faith. Worry is far better placed on those children who have no moral compass at home—they are the ones who will be easily swayed at school.

Is that too tall an order? Many advocates of Christian schools say that we should not expect our children to have to deal with such pressure. You will have to decide regarding your child's personality. Many Christian parents make a conscious decision to be involved in the local public school (notice I said that *they* will be involved, not just their children) in hopes of being "salt and light." You are not sending your children to the wolves if you are walking right in with them. As parents get involved by interacting with staff, teachers, and other parents, their Christian values will be apparent. They can get involved with the PTA; they can go into the class-rooms to help the teachers. Above all, they talk with their children and keep on top of what is going on. You can explain a lot of things from the biblical point of view, and you can head off some problems at the pass.

In the public school, teachers will not all be Christian—that's a given. Some may even be hostile to Christianity. Your child will be taught that evolution is how he came to be—with no mention of God. But a child grounded in the faith through church and home spiritual teaching will be able to discern what is right. One ten-year-old came home after the day's teaching on evolution and told her mom, "You won't believe what the science teacher taught us today! He's crazy!" She knew the truth, and the conversation with her mom helped her to see the big picture—that fine line of not questioning or ridiculing the teacher's authority while still discerning truth from falsehood.

In the younger grades, your child will probably make Halloween decorations and have a Halloween party. In the older grades, they will face health education classes that will allow for freedoms you would not permit. Your child will rub shoulders with people with no moral compasses and will hear words he may have never heard before.

But such is the world in which we live. The best thing to remember is that your children will need your continued involvement and guidance—especially if they go to the public school. Talk to your child about what's going on in class and on the playground. When he mentions a friend, invite that friend over and find out what he's like in your home. Gently help your child through the various situations he faces—keep communicating so the doors stay open for you to walk with him as the years go by. The public school is a tough place, but Christian kids are not victims—they are armed and dangerous by God's grace. They can be an influence for good, even in their own small ways. And so can you.

THE PRIVATE CHRISTIAN SCHOOL

A local Christian school can be a true blessing. Sending your kindergartner into a classroom where God is honored as part of the curriculum, the teacher is a Christian, and the fellow students are from Christian homes will take away many of the flip-flops you feel on that first day of school. In a Christian school, your children learn that God is involved in every part of life—an important life lesson. They will find friends whose families have values similar to yours. They will pray in class. They will have the Bible as a standard part of the curriculum. They will have worship (chapel) services. Often the curriculum is solidly built on the basics because they are not mandated by the government for various peripheral teaching. You may find that the discipline is stricter and more well-enforced.

Often the cost is a key factor in deciding whether your children will attend a Christian school. You are actually paying twice—your real estate taxes support the public school while you will have to pay a separate bill for the Christian school. But even if you can afford it doesn't necessarily mean you must do it. There are other factors to consider, as noted below. If you can't afford it, that may make the decision for you. However, if you're in between and truly feel that God wants you to send your children to the Christian school, then prayerfully look at your budget. You may be able to pare back in some places. Mom might be able to get part-time work while the children are in school in order to offset the cost. Most schools offer financial aid. Sometimes if a parent can work at the school, the school will offer a discount on the tuition. Look into these and other options to see if you can make it affordable.

Christian schooling builds a solid foundation for your children. They come away from even a few years armed with the ability to see God's hand in all aspects of life. The friendships built there, especially at high school age, may last a lifetime. Being surrounded by like-minded peers can also build a solid foundation for social relationships.

It is worthwhile to visit the Christian school(s) available to you. Sometimes a very small school has several grades in one room—perhaps only a few children per grade. One teacher may preside over the entire room. The curriculum may be dependent on the child's ability to work on his own and be self-motivated. There may be little opportunity for extras such as music, art, sports, etc. Other schools, however, are large enough to have classrooms for each grade and extracurricular activities. By all means, take the time to find out how the school is run and assess your child's needs (see the section on Evaluating Schools on page 157).

THE HOMESCHOOL

The segment of the student population that is being homeschooled continues to grow every year. Families become disillusioned with the public schools and, for one reason or another, decide not to attend a Christian school. Homeschooling families must have an intense desire to take on their children's schooling as a full-time job. These parents will tell you that "anyone can do it," and, while true, it takes a mom with initiative and a dad with lots of encouragement and understanding to tackle this task with the best outcome for the children.

The beauty of homeschooling is that your children are in a familiar environment with familiar people. They can progress at their own rate—which is often faster than they would in school. The child avoids the subtle (or not so subtle) grading and classifying that occurs in school. He avoids social cliques and pressures that occur even at early ages. The curriculum can often be covered in half a day, leaving children free to read, work on other activities, go on field trips, etc. You can gear the child's time frame on various subjects—if math is proving to be difficult, a whole day can be spent on it until it sinks in. Such is the flexibility afforded by homeschooling.

Many people wonder about the vague concept of "socialization"—as if socializing is some magic cure of many diseases. Yet it is important for children to learn the skills of getting along with others, sharing, kindness, etc. Many homeschooling families have more than one child, so those basic skills are being taught among siblings. In addition, most home-schooling families attend church, so their children are involved in Sunday school classes and other groups. Most places have homeschooling net-works where families join together for a field trip, drama, music or art classes, or even sports. In short, resources are available to the home-schooling family.

But the parents, especially Mom if she is to be the main teacher, need to realize that this is a big commitment—time-consuming, twenty-four-hours-a-day. It will take organization and creativity—as well as a good dose of self-discipline so that you can keep the children disciplined and on track. Some states require a certain amount of record keeping. Before jumping in, talk to other parents who do it and find out the requirements, the support groups, the places to study, and decide on the curriculum you want to use, etc.

The rewards of schooling your children are enormous. The time you will spend teaching your children will provide precious opportunities to talk with them, model the values you want to teach, answer questions that arise "out of the blue," go on field trips or vacations without bowing to the school schedule—even take a day off now and then just to have some fun. You can spend a day baking in the kitchen and teach fractions with the measuring cups. If your child excels in music, you can schedule lessons during the day and set aside extra practice time. The flexibility home-schooling provides can be a great plus for your children and can build priceless memories as well.

As you look over your options, consider the needs of your child and of your family. Also realize that a decision is not irreversible. You may decide to start your children at home and then move them into the Christian school. You may find that the public school is not working out for one of your children and so you bring her home for a year to help her catch up through your personal attention and instruction. While going back and forth constantly is not good for the children either, take a year at a time and make the best decision you can based on prayer and God's guidance.

It is important to remember that, no matter what schooling option you choose, you as parents are the most important influence on your children's lives. If you are modeling values, morals, and Christian disciplines, your children will build on that foundation. If you are vitally involved in your children's lives and schooling, they will be far better for it. Just because your children are in a Christian school does not mean that you can opt out because everything is being cared for. Your children still need *you*.

EVALUATING SCHOOLS AND THE NEEDS OF YOUR CHILD

If you are fortunate enough to have the option of schools for your child, you will have to make that decision. The best way is to consider your child's needs and to then look carefully at the options that are available.

Remember each child is unique. One of your children may thrive in the public school; another may need the foundation formed at a Christian school. If the options are open and you can afford private schooling, then be flexible.

The best thing you can do is educate yourself about the schools. You may have heard various opinions—good and bad—about both types of school. While talking to parents who have children in these schools is a must, remember to take all opinions with a grain of salt. Talk to several different parents in order to get a balanced view.

Visit each school. Make an appointment to talk with the principal. Ask to be able to sit in on a couple of classroom sessions. Speak to teachers. Observe what is on the walls. Watch the attentiveness of the students. While not all teachers and classrooms are the same, your visit should help you get a general "feel." As you get the atmosphere, think about whether you would want to spend six hours a day for 180 days in that school.

Realize that most schools really do have your children's best interests in mind. Public schools certainly have many types of people vying for control at the highest levels (such as the National Education Association). Many of these people are anti-Christian and their influence can be felt. However, you may find that at your local school, the teachers and parents are working together in their desire to provide what is best for the children. If your community will not stand for certain things (such as the homosexual agenda), chances are the school is not going to go flagrantly against the community. Most of the millions of teachers in the classroom want to give your child the best education possible. They want to teach the basics; they want to see your child succeed. Most elementary schools welcome and invite parental involvement. Ask what opportunities might be available for you to be involved in the school.

If your child excels in a particular area—music, sports, art—see what each school has to offer. A large public school might have a great music program where your child can learn more. But a smaller Christian school might be lacking. On the other hand, the smaller school might offer your son, newly interested in basketball, an opportunity to actually *play* on the school team. In addition, if your child has special needs, a Christian school may not have the funds to provide extra help while the public school often does. On the other hand, you may find that more personalized attention can be given to your special-needs child in a smaller school, and that can offset the need for a special program.

Remember that it is not always the most beautiful facilities that make for the best school. Even exceptionally high standards—good in themselves—may not be the best atmosphere for a child who has to work hard just to get by. Such a school might intimidate him and make it so difficult that he ends up hating school—and perhaps hating learning as well. That would be a high price to pay.

Pray over your children. Ask God to guide you as you make these decisions for them. Ask Him to reveal to you each child's gifts and special abilities. God will do what is best for your child through you as you gather information and then listen to Him.

GETTING YOUR CHILD READY TO BEGIN SCHOOL

Many parents feel that they want to give their child every advantage possible before he or she begins school. But you don't need to feel that your child must master reading, writing, and arithmetic before stepping through the kindergarten room door. But there are several things you *can* do to prepare your child to begin school.

As part of your parenting, you are teaching your child how to interact with adults and with other children. Hopefully, you are disciplining him consistently so that he is learning the difference between acceptable and unacceptable behavior. Being able to relate socially to his peers (understanding kindness, sharing, etc.) and respecting the authority of adults (whether parents or teachers) will go a long way to helping your child be ready for school.

Talk to your child—and listen to her. Teach her the art of conversation as she learns from you how to state an opinion, speak clearly and correctly, express feelings appropriately, etc. When she sees you listening intently when she talks to you, she will learn the importance of listening carefully when someone talks to her. Learning to be quiet and listen is obviously an important skill to prepare your child for school. In addition, help your child learn to listen for a length of time. That doesn't mean parking her in front of the television for long amounts of time, for often television is more fast-paced entertainment than what the average kindergarten teacher will provide. Encourage her to listen to audio tapes of stories. Most libraries loan storybooks with a cassette tape that goes along with the story being read. Better yet, take the time to read aloud to your child. She will learn to sit for a length of time and focus on a task.

Give your child lots of stimulating activities to do with his hands. Right from the start, teach him how to correctly hold a crayon. This will later translate into correctly holding a pencil. Buy children's scissors and let your child cut pictures from magazines. The skill of cutting with scissors, and how to safely handle them, is helpful to know before starting school. Let him mold with clay, fingerpaint, color, draw, use a paintbrush, and practice with glue. All of these skills will make the activities in kindergarten seem familiar and more comfortable.

Help your child develop a curiosity and interest in the world. This curiosity will translate into a love of learning. Go for walks. Help awaken his senses to the sights, sounds, smells, and feel of God's beautiful creation. Talk about whatever questions he has. If he asks a question and you don't know the answer, go to the library and look it up.

Which brings me to the next activity to prepare your child for school—the library. Take your child there regularly. Check out lots of books to enjoy at home. If your child is asking about the pretty birds she sees, go get lots of books about birds. You need not read every word in every book, but allow your child to browse through the books and look at the pictures. The child will learn that the library is a resource place for the answers to just about any question. Teach the child that the library is a fun place—and a place that will provide hours of entertainment in the form of books about faraway places and enchanting stories.

Often the library will have a computer on which your child can learn some of the basics of computer use. If you have a computer at home, purchase some simple learning games. Your child can learn how to manipulate the mouse and move around the screen.

Wrapped around all these activities, you can painlessly teach the basics—alphabet, counting, shapes, colors, size relationships, etc. Have your child find certain letters on a page. While you're driving, play a game of finding things that are various colors. Find items to count while waiting in a restaurant. Make it fun. Don't reprimand your children for not knowing the letters in perfect order right away—after all, learning the alphabet is a very difficult memory task. There is plenty of time to learn and they will be going over and over the basics in kindergarten. There are many ways to creatively teach your children some of the basics that will send them to kindergarten ready to learn more.

Above all, develop your child's curiosity and teach him that learning is fun. Such a child will walk into the kindergarten room able to listen, focus on a task, enjoy the activities, and get along with his peers. That will get your child started on the right path for the many years of school ahead of him.

THE LEARNING CURVE

The day you send your children off to school is not the day your teaching job ends. Up to the point that they walked into kindergarten, you nurtured them, disciplined them, read to them, taught them letters, colors, shapes, and numbers. But your children will still need you every school day of every school year for the years to come. So don't put away your "teacher" hat just yet.

But what *will* be your job? What can you do to help your child during the early years of school?

Your main job is simply to be involved. From the early years, you will want to help your child develop good study habits. From the day he brings home a page of homework, be sure that you communicate the importance of that piece of paper. Provide a place for your child to do his homework— at a desk in a quiet place, or even near you at the kitchen table while you prepare dinner. Sometimes, sit quietly with them and work on your own paperwork. Be there to answer questions. When the job is completed, have him put the paper in a folder and back into his book bag so that it will not be forgotten in the rush of the next morning. Instilling these skills early will make homework easier to bear in the future.

When your child gets older and has long-term projects, help her lay out a schedule of steps to completion and a target date for each step. She can research, write rough drafts, etc., over a period of weeks instead of needing to pull an all-nighter or turn in late and messy work. Again, these skills will carry over into other projects and into daily life.

However, there is a balance. You are working *with* your child, not *for* him. You are helping to train your child, so you need to be willing to pull back and allow him to assume responsibility. This may mean a late paper sometime or homework that gets left at home. Allow your child to learn from his mistakes without always covering for him. There is a fine line between showing that you care and worrying. You can ask your child if he has homework and if it is done—that shows you care while also communicating to him that the responsibility for getting it done, and done well, is entirely his.

What if your child is struggling with a math concept? Try to do what you can to help explain it, but also realize that teachers are perfectly willing to spend extra time with a child who comes with a question. You can help the child pinpoint what she is struggling with so that she has a concrete question to ask the teacher. Instead of, "I don't get this!" she can say, "I understand how to add the fractions, but what do I do when I need to reduce the answer?" Encourage your child to not be afraid to go to the teacher after class or after school for extra help.

Perhaps your child is struggling with reading—a very basic problem considering most of school will involve reading. Realize that not all children will be reading by the end of first or even second grade. You will see some children way ahead in reading level, while others really struggle. Eventually, however, usually by third grade, most children are reading just fine. If your child is having difficulty, you might first consider eyesight. It could be that her lack of interest in reading is because she simply can't see the words clearly. One mother watched her daughter struggle with third-grade reading, and realized that she kept rubbing her eyes while she read. An eye exam showed just enough farsightedness that letters were difficult to distinguish in the smaller print of third-grade level reading books. The problem could be just that basic.

If your child is reluctant, try keying in on topics of interest to encourage reading. If your child loves sports, you can go to the library and check out books at your child's reading level about sports and sports figures. If your child finds that books can give him information he wants, he's more likely to begin reading—even in spite of himself!

If the problem is more severe, you should talk to your child's teacher for insight and then you might want to think about getting a tutor. You might be able to line up someone at the school who can help, or you might want to hire a private tutor. Sometimes that is just the boost your child needs to get over the hump of whatever difficulty he is facing.

What about report cards? It is a problem when parents look at the grades across a report card that cover subjects from math to physical education and expect their child to excel equally in all areas. While the "straight-A" report card is something to be proud of, it is important for parents to realize that the pressure to achieve that can be very detrimental to a child. Why? Look back at your own experience in grade school. There were subjects you loved; there were subjects you dreaded (and probably still do). The ones you loved were easy As or Bs; the others. . .well, you held your breath and hoped for a decent grade. The reason? Not everyone is wired to excel in every area. People have strong points and weak points. You don't expect your accountant to excel in writing and editing, but you do expect him to know how to add. And she will tell you that the math comes easy, but trying to write a letter is a chore.

That all begins in elementary school. Your child will have natural capabilities—things he is good at, and natural liabilities—things he's not so good at. The American education system is well-rounded and expects children to learn the basics across the board. You should expect your child to pay attention and do his best, but *not* to excel in every area. It simply may not be possible for him. For you to pressure him will hurt more than help.

So what can you do? Watch your child. See what she enjoys intensely—what she gravitates toward. The first few report cards will give you a clue—

as will homework assignments and teacher conferences. You will find that your child naturally excels in some areas and struggles in others. It is important for parents to have realistic expectations of their children. You should expect your child to work hard in all areas (not just the "easy" ones), to do very well in the areas of natural ability, and to do the best she can in the other areas. This is where your encouragement and understanding play a vital role. When you've watched your child work hard all semester, struggle but finish the homework, and study for tests, only to bring home a C grade, you should reward the fact that she did her best. However, if your naturally capable child sloughed off on the math homework because it was just too easy and brought home a C, then you might think about some disciplinary action in order to instill a sense of responsibility.

Grades are important, especially when your child gets into high school, for they are considered by colleges. However, in the early years, it is far more important that you develop in your child a perspective on learning that does not focus on merely getting good grades to the detriment of really learning and enjoying school. It is also important that he learn to do his very best so that, no matter what grade he receives, he has the satisfaction that he did all he could. A poor grade may signal that discipline is needed, but it may also signal a need for special help or support in that particular area. Above all, he must know that you love him no matter what.

WIDE ANGLE

To Preschool or Not to Preschool

"Should you send your bright, obviously-ready-for-school youngster to preschool? Waiting for that magic age when your child can attend kindergarten can seem like a long time for parents who see that their child seems 'ready.' So what should you do?

"First, realize that each child is different—avoid comparisons with the neighbor's kids or older brothers and sisters. What is right for one child may be wrong for another. Consider your child's temperament, social skills, personality, and mental development before putting him in a program. Some children really need preschool; others do not. Here are some questions to ask about your three- or four-year-old:

- Is she bored at home?
- Is he isolated from other children?
- Can I give her what she needs at home?
- Is he ready to be left somewhere, away from home and away from me?
- Can I provide the same preschool experience at home?

"Second, consider your motivation. Watch out for pushing your children to perform to a certain standard to meet *your* needs. Many parents try to fulfill their self-esteem through their children. Watch the infamous "Little League fathers" for a bad example of this. Do you want your child to bring glory to you? Or are you genuinely seeking the best for her?

"Don't use preschool merely for "baby-sitting." There are working mothers who *need* child-care services. Be careful, however, that you do not use preschool as an excuse to "get rid" of your child for a few hours each day so you can have free time.

"Third, approach preschool as *enrichment,* not as a necessity. Most children will adjust rapidly and do very well in school if they have not gone to preschool. Don't think that your children are being deprived or that they will be hopelessly behind if they do not have that 'head start.'

"A positive preschool experience can be a real help to children, however. When choosing a preschool, be sure to check out its safety precautions, the teachers and helpers (credentials, personality, and experience), its reputation, its goals and objectives, and other factors. At a good preschool, children can learn. . .

- to get along with other children.
- to play.

- colors, numbers, and 'kindergarten' skills.
- to learn (preparation for school).
- to listen to adults.
- to leave Mommy and Daddy for a while without crying.
- to resolve conflict.

"While there are definite benefits to a child who is ready, it is important for you to realize that *you* can provide most of these opportunities if you use your imagination and take the time. You can. . .

- devote special time to your child, building his self-esteem and confidence.
- teach her the colors, the alphabet, letter sounds, etc.
- teach him how to write with a pencil, use scissors, and other special skills.
- help lengthen her attention span.
- invite other children over to the house to play.
- purchase 'educational' games and toys.
- talk to other parents to get their ideas.

"If your child is ready, preschool can help her mature, learn, and prepare for school. But she won't be hurt by staying at home if you take the time to care for her by talking, reading, listening, playing, and teaching. The time comes so soon when you will be waving your child off to school for an entire day. Don't be in a hurry. Children grow so fast and these days before school starts can be a precious and memorable time for you and your child."
—Dave Veerman, *Parents and Children*

SECTION 10
MIDDLE SCHOOL

"HELP! I'VE GOT A MIDDLE SCHOOLER!"

(YOU MIGHT BE A PARENT OF A MIDDLE SCHOOL STUDENT IF...)

You knew it would happen someday. Your sweet, innocent baby is growing up and you've become the proud parent of a burgeoning teenager. Check out the sure signs below and see if you recognize the wonderful world of middle-school parenthood!

You might be a parent of a middle school student if...

. . .the family-size box of Ritz crackers you bought yesterday is now empty.

. . .your routine kiss good night is suddenly short-circuited by a sign on the door of his room that says in scrawled handwriting: "No Parents Allowed."

. . .the school shoes you bought him or her last week no longer fit this week.

. . .you keep washing the dog every other day thinking it's Fido who smells so ripe.

. . .you plan your family dinner around reruns of *Saved by the Bell* or *Animaniacs* for fear of mutiny.

. . .your sanity rests on securing one of the following phone features: caller ID, call block, or a second line.

. . .you have to drop your child off one block from their destination so their friends don't see them arriving via their parents' car.

. . .you find the pleated slacks you bought your adolescent for Christmas still in the box in July.

. . .you found Amelia Earhart eating lunch with Jimmy Hoffa under the mound of clothes in your child's room last week.

. . .every question you ask your child is first answered with the word, "Huh?"

. . .you can't recall your last family day together that didn't include soccer, baseball, or cheer squad practice.

. . .the majority of the meaningful conversations you and your child have can be summed up with the words: uh-huh, no, or I don't know.

. . .you are wondering why they call them "slumber" parties.

. . .your family calendar has the birthday of each member of Insync circled in red.

. . .you don't know what Insync is.

. . .the child you once knew spends more time at the mall than at home.

If you've suddenly become the absolute authority on absolutely nothing according to your child, you might be the parent of a middle-school student.

Ah! The pleasures of parent-

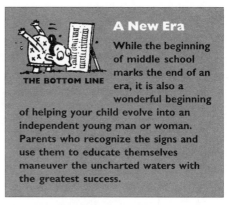

THE BOTTOM LINE

A New Era

While the beginning of middle school marks the end of an era, it is also a wonderful beginning of helping your child evolve into an independent young man or woman. Parents who recognize the signs and use them to educate themselves maneuver the uncharted waters with the greatest success.

hood! You swore the terrible twos were the worst. Then it was the first day of school you thought you'd never get over. But now that you're on the verge of the teenage years, your emotions are touched more than ever! The frustration. The anguish. The worries. The laundry! Middle school can be a trying time for many parents as well as their children. Finding humor in the sometimes-trying situations only a middle-school parent can appreciate can help ease the pain.

CHANGES: IS THIS MY KID?

WHAT'S HAPPENING TO MY BABY?

What was once a respectful, laid-back child has grown into a mouthy sort who can eat twice his or her own body weight at one sitting. What once were family devotions around the fireplace have now become family caucuses where you feel more like a referee than a shepherd. What was once a color-coordinated room complete with sheet set, wallpaper border, and throw pillows is now affectionately referred to as "the pit." What has happened to the house you once knew as home?

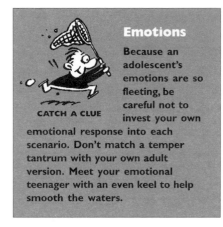

CATCH A CLUE

Emotions

Because an adolescent's emotions are so fleeting, be careful not to invest your own emotional response into each scenario. Don't match a temper tantrum with your own adult version. Meet your emotional teenager with an even keel to help smooth the waters.

Something has invaded your home and that something is called "adolescence."

If you're in the middle of raising a middle-school child, you might be more comfortable recognizing your offspring as a closer relative to the creature from the black lagoon rather than "flesh of my flesh." The changes a middle schooler goes through at this age are remarkable in their complexity and far-reaching in their effects. Let's take a look at the general categories where you can expect a roller coaster of change in the life of a child entering adolescence.

EMOTIONAL

It's not just girls who become emotional at this age. Boys, too, are likely to experience extremes in their emotions as a result of the hormonal Ping-Pong balls ricocheting off every square inch of their bodies. There may be fits of rage over the slightest inconvenience or disappointment. Tears are just at the surface, ready to stream down in anger or inconsolable sadness. And as quickly as these emotions arrive, they mysteriously leave, sometimes in the same instant.

MENTAL

Developmental psychologists who study the growth of the human mind and its potential at various stages in life note this age as a graduation from concrete to abstract ways of thinking. For example, the child who accepted the fact of gravity from reading about Isaac Newton's experience under the apple tree is now the adolescent capable of investigating just how Isaac came up with his theory. At home, you see this

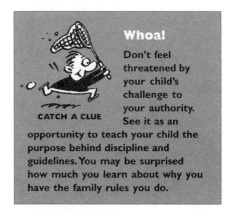

CATCH A CLUE

Whoa!

Don't feel threatened by your child's challenge to your authority. See it as an opportunity to teach your child the purpose behind discipline and guidelines. You may be surprised how much you learn about why you have the family rules you do.

change in the way your child seems to challenge everything you say. It's no longer good enough to explain your rules with, "Because I said so."

SOCIAL

You probably saw this one coming a mile away. In middle school, friends become everything. They have the power to make the day or break the heart. Friendships, while meaningful, are often transient in middle school, fluctuating from week to week. Girls often take an interest in boys like never before and vice versa (albeit usually at a slower pace than the girls).

SPIRITUAL/MORAL

Middle school is a time for questioning that continues into the college years. A faith that has been handed down through family traditions may come into question for the first time: "Is this what I really believe or just what my parents taught me to believe?" Part of their development as embryonic adults is to examine their own views of right and wrong for themselves.

Don't panic when your child "tests" accepted beliefs and practices. Encourage open discussion with your child about morality issues: God, lying, alcohol, sex, abortion, etc. If you've given them a solid foundation to fall back on, chances are they will return to it...but only when they've chosen it for themselves.

PHYSICAL

This is the most obvious area of change and usually the first to come on the scene. Boys' voices begin to crack, girls want to go shopping for their first training bras, and both of them have feet that seemingly grow a size overhaul overnight. Your razors begin to dull at an alarming pace in the girls' shower. And you can't believe how much one kid can sleep. But think how much you'd want to rest, too, if your body were undergoing the overhaul of adolescence.

Above all, protect your child's self-esteem during this most embarrassing time of change. Don't make the mistake of friendly joking about the obvious changes in their bodies—it's serious stuff to the person who has to walk around in that body.

Remember: Though the majority of teens with eating disorders are girls, boys, too, are vulnerable to emotional expression through eating/ weight habits. If you would like more information regarding eating disorders, contact your school counselor's office.

WOW!

Pay Attention

"**When my daughter entered adolescence, the combination of the importance of her friends and her obsession with her appearance caused something devastating in our family. My daughter suffered from an eating disorder for months before I truly realized what was going on. When she was moody and irritable, she said she didn't feel like eating. And with our busier schedule, I didn't notice just how much food she wasn't eating. When she said she was fat, I blew it off and reminded her that she wasn't.**

"**How I wish now that I had paid more attention to the extremes in her moods. Through family counseling, I learned how a young girl can become obsessed with pleasing other people with her appearance. I realize now how distorted her views were about herself and why we needed help.**"
—**Kelly, Phoenix, Arizona**

He will be able to provide you with resources as well as suggestions on local counseling centers.

NOTICING THE OPPOSITE SEX

MARTIAN BOYS AND THE GIRLS FROM VENUS

It's OK

Don't worry if your child seems to have the opposite reaction toward the opposite sex.

CATCH A CLUE

Some teens are late bloomers, especially boys, and their interest in the opposite sex won't come until later. Count your blessings and think of something else to worry about!

If you have a middle-school student, you know that there is a definite change in the way guys and girls relate to each other at this age. And there is a great difference between the sexes in how these changes take place.

In junior high, the girls are typically more aggressive in their romantic pursuits and the guys are often unaware that they're even being pursued! But once they are "caught", they're game for whatever love experiments they can have.

At this time of raging hormones, it's worth explaining the differences between how boys and girls view the opposite sex. For example, guys are sexually stimulated by what their eyes see. Girls are turned on by what their heart feels. Explaining to your young girl the power of physical touch and the visual stimulation of how she is dressed can help her learn the value of restraint. Likewise, teaching a young boy the power of affectionate words and actions and their effect on a girl can keep him from earning the title of a "flirt" or "heartbreaker."

LATE-NIGHT PHONE CALLS AND OTHER INTERESTING THINGS

Establish phone rules early on with your middle-school children and make sure they pass these on to their friends. For example, some families will say no phone calls after a certain time or only on the weekends. Adding a second phone line puts the responsibility on the teen for enforcing these rules—something most middle-school kids are not ready to do!

Encourage mixed groups under your supervision. Have a group of guys and girls over for a special dinner or a pool party with your blessing. This is a great

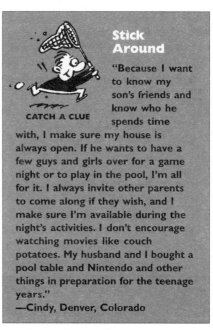

CATCH A CLUE

Stick Around

"Because I want to know my son's friends and know who he spends time with, I make sure my house is always open. If he wants to have a few guys and girls over for a game night or to play in the pool, I'm all for it. I always invite other parents to come along if they wish, and I make sure I'm available during the night's activities. I don't encourage watching movies like couch potatoes. My husband and I bought a pool table and Nintendo and other things in preparation for the teenage years."
—**Cindy, Denver, Colorado**

alternative to sending them off to the mall together to "hang out" or picking them up after a two-hour unsupervised movie.

"If it's out in the open, it's fair game." Many a parent has stumbled onto information about a potential crush while doing the laundry! Finding a diary out in the open or a note wadded in a pocket is fair game for a parent's perusal if you have a reason to be concerned about your child. Swearing true love forever is pretty harmless stuff, but references to sexuality, obsession, or other inappropriate behavior are warning signs that should be heeded and discussed with your middle schooler.

SURVIVING THE FIRST BIG CRUSH

In middle school, relationships are everything. This may be the first time your child experiences a boyfriend/girlfriend relationship. Most relationships during this time last only a few weeks at best and then one or both parties initiate a breakup (usually done through a note or the low blow of a "messenger"). By the time you discover your child is "going with" someone, they may have already broken up! Such is life in middle-school years.

However, someday your son or daughter may get a huge crush on someone and heartache will come to your home. If it hasn't happened in your family yet, hang on. Nearly every kid goes through the cycle of

Some Tips on Surviving a Junior-Size Heartache

CATCH A CLUE 1. **Don't try convincing middle-school boys, or girls, they are not in love. It can't be done! Accept their feelings at face value and help them to maneuver through these new emotions.**
2. **Allow them some space and some time alone. Listening to music in their room is a sanctuary for middle-school students and helps them deal with emotions.**
3. **When the time seems right, arrange a day of fun with their friends—a special play day in the park or a trip to a water park. This will take their mind off of the heartache and remind them there are still plenty of people who love them!**

crush and heartbreak in middle school. Maybe it's the cute girl with freckles down the street who has your son seeing stars. Or maybe it's the blue-eyed boy in math who has your daughter doodling his name over and over again in her notebook. It's the first big crush and your kid is certain this is "the one."

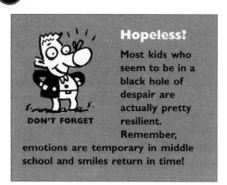

Hopeless?

Most kids who seem to be in a black hole of despair are actually pretty resilient. Remember, emotions are temporary in middle school and smiles return in time!

DON'T FORGET

HAVING "THE TALK"

Most middle-school students have an increased knowledge and experience of sexuality than ever before. But where are they getting their information? TV, the Internet, Howard Stern, their peers, and whatever else they can get their hands on. Shouldn't your perspective as their parents fit in there somewhere? Absolutely! But what do you say and when do you say it?

Some Tips on "The Talk"

1. Some basic biology and understanding of sexuality should come way before middle-school age. Most experts agree grade school is not too early to start.

2. Don't try to cram in all the lifetime lessons you've learned about sexuality and morality in one sitting. Think of "the talk" as a long series of discussions with your teen...driving to school, eating lunch, hanging out on a Sunday afternoon. Make sure he or she knows you're willing to talk or answer any questions anytime.

3. Be honest and open. It's okay to be uncomfortable—attempting to cover

up your nervousness will only make it worse! Teenagers know when you're faking it. Be real and approachable even if you're nervous.

Some Issues Your Teen Might Want in "The Talk" (But Is Too Afraid to Ask):

- When can I start dating?
- What should I look for in a girlfriend/boyfriend?
- How did you know you were in love with Mom/Dad?
- Do you believe in love at first sight?
- What is safe sex?
- Is sex okay if I use birth control/protection during intercourse?
- Why wait until I'm married for sex?

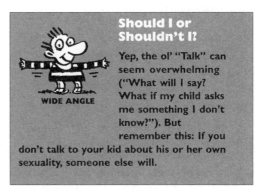

WIDE ANGLE

Should I or Shouldn't I?

Yep, the ol' "Talk" can seem overwhelming ("What will I say? What if my child asks me something I don't know?"). But remember this: If you don't talk to your kid about his or her own sexuality, someone else will.

- Won't my friends think I'm stupid if I'm the only virgin left?
- When will I know I'm ready for sex?
- What do you think about abortion?
- What if I experiment with sex before I'm married?
- How can I get a sexually transmitted disease? What are the diseases like? What about AIDS?
- Will you forgive me if I've already messed up? (or if I mess up?)

TEN REASONS TO TEACH ABSTINENCE UNTIL MARRIAGE

1. Birth control/protection is not foolproof against pregnancy.
2. Birth control/protection does not protect against many sexually transmitted diseases, including AIDS.
3. Safe sex basically advocates Russian roulette for your child. Would you feel comfortable about encouraging them to drive a car at top speed that braked properly only nine out of ten times (the best hypothetical odds)?
4. Putting your daughter on the pill because "she's

WIDE ANGLE

Treasured Moments

"One of the times I will treasure most as a parent was when we introduced the idea of purity to our son. When he neared graduation from middle school, my wife and I took him out to his favorite place for dinner and we laughed, shared, and had a great time. At the table, we gave him a silver ring with a cross in the middle. We explained it was a gift symbolizing his personal commitment to purity—a gift he would someday give to a very special girl. Fortunately, there were many previous occasions when he and I discussed morality and God's plan for sexuality. But that night's focus was on purity—it completed the picture for him and drew us closer together."
—Robert, San Diego, California

going to be sexually active anyway" is a cop-out. Would you hand her a needle if she was "going to do drugs anyway"?

Mum's the Word?

"Unfortunately, the message about sexuality that I got from my parents went something like: 'Sex is a nasty subject that you should never think about or talk about. And you should save it for someone you really love someday.' Give me a break!"
—James, Lewisville, Texas

WOW!

5. Teaching safe sex muddles your rationale for maintaining other boundaries for your teens. If you aid their participation in an emotionally and physically harmful activity, what legitimacy do you have for prohibiting drinking, drug use, stealing, etc.?

6. Premarital sex cheapens their sexual experience in marriage...comparison, threat of disease, haunting memories, etc.

7. They'll grow out of their curiosity stage, but some scars remain. Sexually transmitted diseases like herpes-1 are lifelong diseases without a cure. AIDS can hide dormant in the body's system for as long as ten years.

8. No teenager is fully prepared for the emotional investment and personal commitment sexual intimacy is meant to convey.

9. No parent is ever fully prepared for the possibility of becoming a grandparent with her own teenage child.

10. The safest sex is no sex until you're in a marriage relationship.

SHOULD I LET MY KID GO TO THE SCHOOL DANCE?

AND OTHER QUESTIONS YOU'VE NEVER HAD TO ANSWER BEFORE

Depending on the activity, use the following as a guide to your decision-making.

Questions to Ask About Activities Your Child Wants to Attend:

1. Will there be adult chaperones present?
2. Where exactly is the party/activity?
3. Do you have rides both ways or do I need to drive you?
4. Who is invited to this activity?
5. What activities are planned at the party? (games, cookout, etc.)
6. Do you need spending money? Can the family afford this activity? Can you?
7. Will you have enough time to do this activity and your homework, piano practice, etc.?
8. Will this activity conflict with scheduled family time?
9. Are you too tired/busy to fit this in?

IT'S A MATTER OF TRUST

Students at this age ache to be more independent of their parents and rightfully so. They are emerging into the process of adulthood. However, independence is a privilege, not a right, and must be earned. In middle school, it's wise to begin training your child to understand how trust is built and broken when it comes to independence.

WHEN TRUST IS BROKEN

Discipline, when properly applied, is meant to teach, not to punish. Restricting a child from an activity

WIDE ANGLE

Be Careful

"Some days, when I come home from work, I'm bombarded with questions from my daughter about spending the night with so-and-so or the birthday party on Friday night. Many times I am simply too tired to deal with her insistence. So I give in and say yes, sometimes against my better judgment. But I've learned that if I take the time to get more information about the activity at hand, it's easier to make my decision and stick to my guns. We go over a few simple questions to see if the activity meets the needed 'criteria.' If so, it's a 'yes.' If there isn't enough information or a conflict shows up, it's either 'no' or 'wait.' Of course, my daughter rolls her eyes and says, 'Oh, no, not the list again,' but I feel like I'm helping her to make her own decisions someday. Plus, it helps me not to be arbitrary in my decisions."
—**Stressed-out mom no more, Plano, Texas**

shouldn't be seen as punishment. It is a message to your young teen that says: Independence is not automatic; it must be earned. If a student is not mature enough to function independently (for example, sneaks out of the house at a slumber party), then you must discipline her until she can learn to discipline herself. With the slumber party example, "No slumber parties for awhile" might be your response. When a child learns that her future independence is at risk when tempted to buck the system, bucking the system doesn't seem like so much fun.

However huge the mistake, trust can be rebuilt. And every middle-school student will need a second and third chance to get it right. The key is to rebuild slowly. Don't be too quick to give in just to make things easier and quieter around the house.

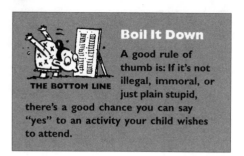

Boil It Down

THE BOTTOM LINE

A good rule of thumb is: If it's not illegal, immoral, or just plain stupid, there's a good chance you can say "yes" to an activity your child wishes to attend.

Chances are, your child won't learn anything from sweeping it under the rug. But don't hold onto grudges either by refusing to allow trust a chance to rebuild between you.

Perhaps one of the best ways to convey what is most important in raising an adolescent is to begin with what kids don't need. Many parents feel pressured into the responsibilities of parenthood at this time and need some relief from the self-imposed expectations.

WHAT MIDDLE SCHOOLERS DON'T NEED:

- They don't need perfect parents who have the best and wisest thing to say for every occasion. No such person exists anyway.
- They don't need parents who never make mistakes and always know how to handle every situation. You're expected to make your share of mistakes, just like you expect your child to mess up, too.
- They don't need parents who are not honest about their insecurities as a parent. After all, every parent is a novice each time they maneuver a child through adolescence. And so is the child.

- They don't need parents who can't admit when they are wrong. Modeling confession and asking for forgiveness are valuable lessons parents shouldn't withold from their children.

DON'T FORGET

Failure Is Sometimes Good

Sometimes the best lessons in life are learned more through failure than success.

WHAT EVERY MIDDLE SCHOOLER NEEDS

Grace

A middle schooler's body is his own worst enemy. They get bumps and welts where they once had smooth, rosy cheeks. Their feet and underarms smell funny and unsightly hair is appearing in the strangest places. Schoolwork is becoming more and more de-manding. And the pressures and temptations in the school hall-ways are more intense than ever.

Watch Your Mouth

"Let your conversation be always full of grace. . ."
(Colossians 4:6)

THE BIBLE SAYS

In the midst of this clumsy, awkward stage in life, there is likely no greater candidate for needing a heaping spoonful of grace than a middle schooler.

Giving your child a second, third, and fourth time to get it right is the best gift you can give them. Accept their sometimes inexplicably irrational emotions without responding with your own emotional tirade. Above all, draw from the wealth of grace you've experienced throughout your lifetime and share it with your child.

Boundaries

To complement the gift of grace, the blessing of boundaries is a must. After all, who can fully appreciate grace without knowing firm boundaries? You can always tell a parents' love for their children by their investment in boundaries. The parent who doesn't care is the overly permissive parent with no restrictions on their child. So, don't get weary in the battle of toeing the line on your convictions. Enforce the curfews, guidelines, and rules in your home with consistency and fairness.

Home

Blended families, single parents, and more and more homes where the grandparents assume the parenting role are part of the cross section of modern student life. With these odd configurations, problems with recognizing authority and understanding family roles begin to surface.

Whatever your own family configuration, your efforts to provide stability, foundation, and refuge in your home are crucial to your child's healthy development. Home is where the majority of education takes place when it comes to social, spiritual, and emotional adjustment. What is your child learning in your home?

SELF-ESTEEM

"Why am I not as pretty as Susan?" "Why did Kevin make the football team and I didn't?" "I'm no good at anything."

At a time when a child is hardest on himself/herself, and his or her peers are often no better, your child needs to be bolstered in your home. A child who bases his or her own self-esteem on what talents he or she possesses is destined for a shaky self-concept. One of your roles as a parent is to reinforce a child's inherent self-worth that is based on who he is, not what he does. In middle school, as in life, talent and good looks are fleeting and can get a person only so far. What messages are you reinforcing in your child about his self-esteem? Does he know you love him regardless of his grades or his place on the team?

Influence

More and more surveys reveal that although many don't receive information about drugs/alcohol or sexuality at home, most students wish they did.
Sure, they act like you are the authority on nothing. But they really want to
hear from parents with wisdom and experience on subjects that matter
most to teens.

One way you can use your role as a parent to its greatest advantage is
to double-team your child with
other adults who foster positive
influence. Involving your family
in a local church or para-church
ministry is a sure-thing investment. Healthy adult leadership
in these ministries will reinforce the same messages they
are learning at home about positive lifestyle and add more credibility to
your messages. "It's not just Mom saying so" is a powerful reinforcement.

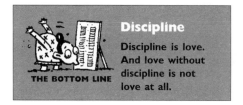

Discipline

THE BOTTOM LINE

Discipline is love.
And love without
discipline is not
love at all.

WHAT PARENTS OF MIDDLE SCHOOLERS NEED

There are some basic needs every parent of middle-school children have.
These needs are common bonds between all parents of adolescents and
speak to every family on a variety of levels.

Positive Images

This generation has made the news headlines more often for acts of
violence than for its acts of benevolence. Stories like the school shootings
that rage across our nation frighten parents everywhere. "That could be my

child!" Negative images of teenagers are plentiful. But they're not entirely accurate as a general description of adolescence today.

Focusing on the positive images and examples of healthy teenagers can alter your perspective on your own child and aid your opinion of teenagers in general. Remind yourself of positive stories of teens raising money for charity or teens involved in community service, and you'll begin to see your attitude change. When you hear about a teen involved in a positive lifestyle, tell yourself, "That could be my child" and strive toward that positive image. Your kid can be an extraordinary teen, too.

Mentors

Every parent needs a mentor parent who has seen the light at the end of the tunnel. An older couple with kids in college can be a wonderful resource for you as you deal with the uncharted waters of adolescence. You can find couples through work, church, or even your own social circles. Developing a mentoring relationship provides you a sounding board to vent your frustration and get free advice from someone who's been there, done that.

Open Eyes and Open Ears

Every parent needs to be on their guard for warning signs of trouble in their teen's life. Peer pressure in middle school is only the beginning of a lifetime of greater temptations. Although time will be fleeting in both middle and high school, secure times of open communication with your teen early on. Pay attention to changes in sleeping patterns, signs of depression, missed curfews, lies, etc. Most of it is typical teenage behavior. However, follow your instincts as a parent and don't hesitate to act before it's too late if you suspect your teen is becoming involved in suspicious or harmful behavior.

Patience

This may well remain at the top of every parent's wish list. But be careful what you wish for! You have to go through trying experiences in order to learn patience. While it's true that teens come out on the other side of adolescence as changed people, hopefully parents do, too. Be sure you are working on your own character development during the trying times of adolescence. Allow the hard times to shape you and not defeat you. Ask for help from your spouse, peer support groups, and through prayer.

THE CHANGE: WHAT TO EXPECT FROM YOUR MIDDLE SCHOOLER

Change	Result	Your Reaction
Emotional	Mood swings; roller-coaster experiences; hormonal overload; tantrums; crying for no reason	Don't react to outburst; don't contribute your own emotional outburst
Mental	Move from concrete to abstract thought; wants more than just the facts; challenges the "why" behind rules; questioning	Don't take it personally; consider and express why you have and enforce your family rules
Social	Relationships become everything; relationships are formed independent of	Secure family time on calendar; help them choose positive influences; encourage

	Mom and Dad; opposite sex becomes prominent; less family time; more opportunities/activities, crushes/heartaches	supervised opposite-sex activities
Spiritual/Moral	Move from concrete to abstract ideas of faith/morality; independent ideas; questions faith; questions previously accepted rules	Don't panic; help them think things through; provide a solid moral/spiritual foundation
Physical	Percolating glands and raging hormones; voice changes; stature; increased sexuality; clumsy; acne; awkwardness	Inform your child about responsibilities of sexuality; don't make fun of or embarrass them

SECTION 11
HIGH SCHOOLER

"WHAT HAPPENED TO MY CUTE LITTLE BABY?"

CHANGES IN HIGH SCHOOL

High-school-age kids face tremendous pressures from outside sources as well as from within their own bodies. These pressures are bound to produce changes—whether *you're* ready for them or not. When you notice some of the following changes occurring in your son or daughter, you've got two choices. You can either mourn the loss of your "cute little baby" or you can welcome the arrival of a young adult.

EXPERIMENTATION

There's a world of possibilities awaiting your teenager. Chances are, she's eager to explore them all. Some experimentation is harmless. For example, your daughter may ask you to start calling her by her middle name. Some experimentation is a little radical and disconcerting. If you've ever seen a teenager with her hair dyed a color not found in nature, you know what we're talking about. Some experimentation is dangerous. This would include everything from alcohol to sex, from drugs to joining a gang.

Accept the fact that your child is going to experiment. Learn to tolerate (and perhaps even encourage) harmless experimentation, while at the same time discouraging harmful experimentation.

SEPARATION

Your teenager is going to try to distance himself from you, and there's not much you can do about it. He needs to figure out who he is, apart from you. Quite often, he needs his own space in which to do his own figuring.

It's not that he doesn't need you anymore; it's that his need is taking a different form. He still needs your love and support, but he doesn't need your protection as much as he used to. Instead, he needs your recognition and acceptance of his burgeoning maturity.

The worst thing you can do is take your child's separation urges personally. The best thing you can do is give him plenty of room and remind him often that you're always there for him.

MOODINESS

Hormones are running wild in your teenager's body, occasionally taking on a life of their own. The body changes that these hormones produce will likely be quite noticeable to you and the rest of your family. Beyond the physical evidence of zits and body hair, though, you'll notice some emotional changes in your child. Wild mood swings, from delirium to depression and back again in the course of a day are par for the teenage course. We're not suggesting that living with a hormone-soaked adolescent will be a walk in the park. However, we can guarantee that the situation is both temporary and survivable.

CHALLENGES

More and more, you'll find that your teenager no longer accepts your wisdom at face value. Words and phrases like "Why?" "How do you know?" and "You don't know everything!" will start to crop up in your conversations. It's not necessarily rebellion that's rearing its head; more likely, it's independent thought.

It's also a fact-finding mission. Like it or not, your teenager has entered the marketplace of ideas. Yours isn't the only voice he's hearing anymore. Yours isn't the only opinion he's considering. In order to discover the truth for himself, your teenager may need to challenge everything he hears (or at least everything *you* say—parents tend to bear the brunt of their child's challenging phase).

Your best preparation for these challenges is to know what you believe and why you believe it. If you're able to explain your beliefs so that your teenager is able to recognize the wisdom in them, so much the better.

A PEEK INSIDE

WHAT MAKES YOUR HIGH SCHOOLER TICK?

If little girls are made of sugar and spice and everything nice, and little
boys are made of frogs and snails
and puppy dog tails, what are
teenagers made of? Depends on
who you ask. A doting parent will
tell you one thing; a beleaguered
teacher will tell you another.
Though there may not be one
recipe for all teenagers, there are
a few ingredients that are common to most of them.

They're Changing

"Our son's biggest rite of passage: the day he answered the phone and was *not* asked if he was his mom."

—Kendra Smiley, member of the Understanding Your Teenager Seminar team

RESTLESSNESS

Teenagers are trapped in a netherworld between childhood and adulthood—too old to be treated like kids, too young to be treated like grown-
ups. As you may or may not remember, it's not a comfortable place to exist.
Most teenagers anxiously await the day when the world recognizes their
maturity. They're restlessly making their way toward adulthood.

Usually their journey is marked by milestones along the way. First, they can't wait until they're old enough to date. Next, they can't wait until they're old enough to drive. Then they can't wait until they're old enough to graduate. Finally, they can't wait until they're old enough to live on their own. In short, most teenagers are in a perpetual rush to get to the next stage in life.

This generally restless spirit is matched by a more specific restlessness that comes from teenagers' rapidly changing bodies. Growth spurts, hormone surges, and a seemingly endless supply of energy make it difficult for many teenagers to sit sill or focus on one subject for more than a short period of time. The sooner you realize and accept this as a parent, the more of your sanity you'll be able to hold onto.

FEAR AND UNCERTAINTY

Though most teenagers aren't likely to admit to being afraid, they are. Specifically, they're afraid of the adult world and the changes it brings. This is especially true of older teens, those who have started thinking about high school graduation.

For kids who have gotten the hang of it, living the teenage life is a breeze. The responsibilities are light and the rewards are unbeatable. Despite the restrictions of home and school, there is a tremendous freedom in being a teenager. The adult world, on the other hand, is chock-full of decisions, responsibilities, and bills. What kid in his right mind wouldn't dread those things?

PEER PRESSURE

Some people would have you believe that peer pressure is the archenemy of all teenagers and the source of everything wrong with kids today. It's not. In fact, some studies have shown that parental influence is actually much stronger than peer pressure!

That's not to say that peer pressure isn't a force to be reckoned with. It is. Your kids *will* be influenced by their friends, the things they watch on TV, and the things they see in their everyday lives—to a degree. The degree that kids are affected by these things, though, will depend on how many other influences are around to counteract them. If you remain a steady, stabilizing influence in your teenager's life, peer pressure won't be much of an issue.

INVINCIBILITY

Many teenagers are oblivious to physical danger. The prospect of being seriously injured, regardless of the activity, is not something that crosses most kids' minds. Because they're in the prime of their lives, teenagers believe they're capable of escaping any dicey situation that comes their way. You see this fearless attitude in the way they drive, the way they skate, and the risks they take in other areas of life. Unfortunately, it usually takes an injury (or worse) to them or someone close to them to challenge their feelings of invulnerability. Until that happens, you're in for your share of gray hairs and heart palpitations.

"I'VE GOTTA BE ME...!"

THE QUEST FOR IDENTITY

"Who am I?"

For a teenager, that's a tough question. In fact, most kids spend their entire teenage years trying to answer it. Though you may not be able to give your teenager the answer she's looking for, you can support her in her quest. Here's how.

Encourage your teenager to form his own opinions.

Want to surprise your teenager? Turn to him during the evening news and ask him for his thoughts regarding a specific hot-button issue in society today. Once he recovers from the shock of having his opinion sought after, your teen may surprise you with some thoughtful insight.

When was the last time you asked your teenager how he feels about a controversial topic? When was the last time you allowed him to share an opinion that you disagree with—without trying to change his mind? When was the last time you gave serious thought to a point your teenager made? These are all important steps in the adolescent development process. They are also extremely effective ways of letting your child know that you recognize his burgeoning maturity.

Be patient as your teenager tries on different attributes, interests, and beliefs.

As the parent of a teenager trying to find her identity, you're going to see some strange things. Some of your child's choices will make you laugh; others will make you wince. Some will appeal to you; others will appall you. However, unless your child is courting danger or personal harm in her choices, give her some room to experiment with herself. Let her discover what works for her—not just in her appearance, but in her personality and belief system as well. She may not make the choices you would make for her, but that's okay. She may even embarrass you on occasion, but that's okay, too. A little embarrassment now is a small price to pay for a well-adjusted, independent-thinking adult tomorrow.

Do your best to disguise your amusement, disappointment, irritation, and frustration at your teenager's various guises. Sooner or later she's bound to find one that works for her—and one that you'll be able to live with as well.

Remember your own youthful experimentation.

Before you go overboard worrying about your teenager's quest for identity, think back to your own formative years. Chances are, you weren't much different from your child. (If you need help, ask your parents to refresh your memory concerning some of the ill-advised choices you made as a teen.)

Empathize with what your teenager is going through. If you're feeling especially open and vulnerable, share some of your more embarrassing identity experiments with your child. (Photographic evidence of your youthful follies would be an especially valuable visual aid.) Your ability to laugh at yourself may make it easier for your teenager to deal with the taunting and teasing he'll likely encounter as he searches for an identity. You may be surprised at the bond that forms as a result of such an encounter.

Don't be stingy with praise and encouragement.

Sooner or later your teenager is going to hit on some things that work for her. When she does, make sure you let her know it. When you see smart choices, impressive changes, or obvious signs of maturity in your teenager's life, tell her about it. Encourage other members of your family to do the same thing. Always be on the lookout for praiseworthy developments in your child's maturation process.

FAITHFUL COMPANIONS

DEALING WITH YOUR TEENAGER'S FRIENDS

You're not going to like every friend your teenager hangs out with. That's a given. But you're not totally helpless when it comes to influencing your child's friendships. Here are a few suggestions you might consider.

Make an effort to get to know your teenager's friends.
Encourage your kids to bring their friends around. Make your home a place where kids will want to hang out. When kids are around, engage them in small talk. Find out what's going on in their lives. You may be surprised by what you learn. You may find

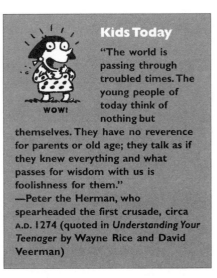

Kids Today

WOW!

"The world is passing through troubled times. The young people of today think of nothing but themselves. They have no reverence for parents or old age; they talk as if they knew everything and what passes for wisdom with us is foolishness for them."
—Peter the Herman, who spearheaded the first crusade, circa A.D. 1274 (quoted in *Understanding Your Teenager* by Wayne Rice and David Veerman)

that when you get to know them, your teenager's friends aren't anything like you thought they were.

Watch for warning signs.

There's a difference between giving your teenager the benefit of the doubt when it comes to friends and turning a blind eye to his social life. Always keep your eyes open for signs that your child is involved in dangerous or harmful activities. If you notice increased secretiveness or moodiness, if you catch him sneaking around, or if you start to hear rumors about things that are going on, don't hesitate to act.

Confront carefully.

Many kids are extremely loyal to their friends. An attack on the people they hang out with is seen as an attack on them. That's why it's important for you to avoid name-calling, generalizing, and stereotyping when you talk to your teenager about his friends.

Your best bet is to focus on specific behavior that you've witnessed. Then, rather than telling your teenager how much *you* dislike the friend's actions, get his perspective. For example, instead of saying, "I don't want you hanging around with foul-mouthed people like Michael," ask, "Does it ever bother you when Michael talks the way he does around your family?" Not only will you get your teenager's input on his friend's behavior, you may also prompt him to do something about it.

STEADY DATES, UNSTEADY PARENTS

BOYFRIENDS AND GIRLFRIENDS

Unless you plan to forbid your child from dating until she graduates from college, you're going to have to deal with the specter of teenage dating. The fact is, your little "baby" is going to want to fraternize with the opposite sex—on a regular basis. And that presents all kinds of challenges—and opportunities—for you. Here are some suggestions for making the most of a difficult situation.

Make the boyfriend or girlfriend comfortable around your family.
If you're like most parents, you're probably going to feel some resentment toward the people your child dates. That's okay. A little parental jealousy is perfectly normal. You'll also probably find yourself thinking that no one is good enough for your child. That's also a perfectly normal emotion.

What's *not* perfectly normal, though, is allowing those feelings to drive a wedge between you and the person your teenager is dating. Think of it this way: The more comfortable your child's boyfriend or girlfriend is around your family, the more time the two of them are likely to spend with you. The more time they spend with you, the better chance you'll have to see the inner workings (for better or worse) of their relationship.

Who knows? In time, you may even come to view your teenager's significant other less as an interloper and more as—dare we say it?—a member of your family.

Always be ready with a listening ear.

The ups and downs of a relationship can stir up some pretty powerful emotions in teenagers. They need someone they can talk to. To become that person for your child, you'll need to learn to bite your tongue occasionally and just listen. Forget about your role as a parent and commiserate with her as someone who's also struggled with teenage dating relationships.

It would be extremely helpful for you to learn to open up to your teenager. If you want your kid to be honest with you, it's only fair that you be honest with her. Share some of your own experiences (good and bad) with dating and relationships. Of course, you don't want to share more than your child is equipped to handle. Just let her know that you know a little about what she's going through.

BEYOND THE BIRDS AND THE BEES

SEX AND YOUR TEENAGER

You're the best sex expert your child could ever hope to have. Do you *really* want her going anywhere else to find out what she needs to know? In order to be the adviser your teenager needs, you must learn to talk openly and frankly about sex. It may take some work (and perhaps even a bit of study) on your part, but it will be worth the effort.

Talk about it often.

The "sex" talk shouldn't be a one-time discussion, but an ongoing dialogue. Use everyday information, such as a statistic on teenagers with sexually transmitted diseases or a news report on teenage mothers, to prompt communication on the topic. Knowing where babies come from isn't enough for your teenager. Help her become acquainted with the long-term physical, social, emotional, and practical implications of sex.

Let your teenager know that you have faith in her.

Earning a parent's trust is a big deal for most kids. Chances are, if your teenager believes you trust her, she will be less likely to do something to risk that trust. That's not to say you should have blind faith in your child's ability to make the right decisions twenty-four hours a day. That's just asking for trouble. But if you give your teenager a sense of responsibility for her own sexual purity (and your trust), you'll probably find that she will rise to the challenge.

Pray.

Sex is a tremendous temptation, especially for teenagers. All the warnings, pleas, and encouragement in the world may not make a difference when the moment of truth arrives. That's why it's important to turn your teenager's situation over to a Higher Authority. Ask the Lord to provide guidance and strength for your child to resist sexual temptation.

BRIDGING THE GENERATION GAP

UNDERSTANDING YOUTH CULTURE

In order to understand your teenager, you have to know something about the culture in which he is growing up—the messages that bombard him every day and the people and things that entertain him. You need to do a little cultural exploration. Be warned: We can give you tips on how to familiarize yourself with today's youth culture, but we can't guarantee that you'll like—or even be able to tolerate—what you find. That's why they call it a generation gap.

Acquaint yourself with the things your teenager listens to and watches.

When was the last time you listened to one of your teenager's CDs? When was the last time you watched a video that he wanted to see? How well do you know your child's taste in music and movies? Try familiarizing yourself with the things your child enjoys. It may give you some insight into his character. At the very least, it will give you common ground for conversation.

Listen to what teenagers are talking about.

When your teenager has friends over, keep your ears open. Find out what kinds of things they're interested in, what they spend their time talking about. This is *not* to suggest that you eavesdrop on private conversations. If you don't give your teenager and her friends the privacy they want, they won't be spending much time around you. However, if your child and her friends feel comfortable talking in front of you, learn to be an observant (but not obvious) listener.

Take advantage of any common interests you share.

It's a big world out there, filled with all kinds of interesting things to do. If you look hard enough, you're bound to find some activities that you and your teenager both enjoy. Maybe you're both in-line skaters. Maybe you both root for the Chicago Cubs. Maybe you both get a kick out of watching cheesy science fiction movies. Whatever common ground you share, take advantage of it. Ask your teenager to teach you some tricks on your rollerblades. Surprise him with tickets to a game. Rent *Plan 9 from Outer Space* some night when you're both going to be home. Even the tiniest shared interest can serve as a springboard to better communication with, and a better understanding of, your teenager.

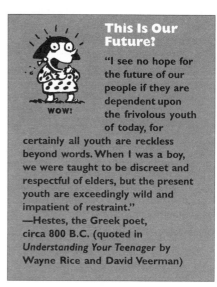

This Is Our Future?

WOW!

"I see no hope for the future of our people if they are dependent upon the frivolous youth of today, for certainly all youth are reckless beyond words. When I was a boy, we were taught to be discreet and respectful of elders, but the present youth are exceedingly wild and impatient of restraint."
—Hestes, the Greek poet, circa 800 B.C. (quoted in *Understanding Your Teenager* by Wayne Rice and David Veerman)

Talk to other adults.

Try as you might, you can't become an expert on every aspect of the youth culture. The field is too broad. That's why it's a good idea to develop a network of helpful "correspondents." Open up lines of communication with church youth workers, high school teachers, and other parents. Pick their brains concerning the things that affect your child. With a broad range of expertise to draw on, you'll be better-equipped to understand the world your teenager lives in.

Recognize that teenage interests are ever-changing.

If your teenager adopts a style, attitude, or trend that confuses, embarrasses, or irritates you, take heart. Chances are, the infatuation will be fleeting. Kids' tastes are fickle. What's hot today is hopelessly dated tomorrow. There are too many things vying for your kids' attention and emulation for them to concentrate too long on one particular look or persona. The best thing you can do is learn to be patient and ride out the waves of fashion and trends.

Don't try to become a part of it.

Learning about youth culture is one thing; adopting it for yourself is quite another. There's nothing shameful or outdated about being a parent. Don't be afraid to act like one. Don't try to be hip if you're not. Don't pretend to enjoy things that you don't enjoy. Every generation deserves its own unique culture. Let your teenager enjoy his.

POST-MISTAKE RECOVERY

HELPING YOUR KIDS THROUGH TOUGH TIMES THEY'VE BROUGHT ON THEMSELVES

If your teenager isn't making her share of mistakes, chances are she's not living life to the fullest. Mistakes are a part of life. So is the process of dealing with them. If you can help your teenager learn to take responsibility for and then recover from her mistakes, you'll be equipping her with the skills she needs to become a healthy, productive adult.

Make sure your teenager fully understands what's been done.
Kids almost always know when they've done something wrong. Look closely enough and you'll usually see the guilt written on their faces. However, they don't always know *why* certain things are such a big deal to adults.

Your job is to help your teenager recognize the full consequences for her actions. For example, if your teenager has been caught in a lie, you need to help her understand the devastating effects lying has on a person's reputation. If she's done something foolish or careless, you need to help her recognize the danger she posed to herself or to others.

Your teenager may accuse you of beating a dead horse or of rubbing salt in a wound. That's why it's important for you to separate the discussion about consequences from the punishment process. Take the necessary disciplinary action. When that's over, sit down with your child to calmly discuss the consequences of what she did.

Forgive and forget.

The next time you get into an argument with your teenager, you're going to be tempted to throw past mistakes in her face to help make your point. Resist the temptation. If your child has taken responsibility for a mistake and accepted the consequences, she's earned the right not to have that mistake used against her.

To find a model of the kind of forgiveness your teenager deserves, you need look no further than God's words in Jeremiah 31:34: "For I will forgive their wickedness and will remember their sins no more."

FIGHTING THE GOOD FIGHT — HELPING YOUR KIDS KEEP THEIR VALUES

Beyond showing them love and keeping them safe, the best thing you can do for your children is equip them with God-honoring values. It's not an easy task. We live in a world that is apathetic at best and antagonistic at worst to those who try to maintain godly values.

Few things are viewed in black-and-white terms anymore. Shades of gray are everywhere. People who use words like *right* and *wrong* are labeled "narrow-minded" and accused of trying to impose their morality on others.

It's a tough environment for teenagers who are trying to live their Christian faith. Here are some ways you can equip your teenager with solid values and prepare him for the challenges that lie ahead.

Model the values you want your child to keep.

"Do as I say and not as I do" is not an effective approach when it comes to influencing teenagers. It never has been and it never will be. If you want to influence the way your kids think and act, you've got to do it through your actions. Don't try to convince your child of the importance of taking care of his body with a cigarette in your hand. Don't try to preach the importance of honesty and integrity if you're the type of person who will do anything to get ahead in life.

Teenagers have sharp senses when it comes to spotting phoniness and hypocrisy. Once you've been caught trying to pass off values that you yourself don't keep, you'll find that your influence in your teenager's life will diminish significantly.

If you want to be the kind of person your teenager will listen to when the conversation turns to values, you may need to make some drastic, and difficult, changes in your life. The good news is that when your teenager sees how committed you are to the values you hold, he will be more likely to turn to you when he too is struggling with those values.

Show your teenager the practical nature of values.

Always be prepared to answer the questions "Why?" and "Why not?" when you talk with your teenager about values. Help her understand that values have tangible benefits. For example, the person who abstains from sex before marriage doesn't have to worry about unwanted pregnancy or sexually transmitted diseases. Likewise, the person who commits herself to honest communication never has to worry about being caught in a lie.

Examples (both positive and negative) from your own life and the lives of people you know will go a long way toward helping your teenager recognize the practical nature of values.

Make biblical and value-based conversations part of your everyday routine.

We're not talking about in-depth Bible studies here. We're talking about making Scripture as much a topic of casual conversation as the weather. Furthermore, we're not talking about launching into a dissertation on the nature of grace every morning at breakfast. We're talking about relating biblical principles to everyday areas of life.

We're talking about opening up to your teenager and sharing your own triumphs and struggles with biblical values. For example, if you faced a situation at work in which you were tempted to lie—but resisted—casually mention it to your teenager. But don't do it with a "Look how holy I am" attitude. Be honest about how hard it was for you to resist the temptation. Let your teenager know exactly what happened as a result of your honesty and how you feel about it now.

AT THE TABLE

WHAT TO DO ABOUT YOUR TEENAGER'S DIET

One of the earliest forms of independence your teenager will experience is the freedom to eat what he wants. Whether it's due to your busy schedule or his, chances are your child will often be left to his own devices at mealtime. Here are some steps you can take to make sure that your teenager's eating habits aren't a lost cause.

Limit junk food as much as possible.
Trying to ban junk food completely from your teenager's diet would be about as effective as trying to ban facial blemishes. Like acne, junk food is part of a teenager's everyday life. What you *can* do is limit the necessity for junk food. If you have meals prepared for your child every night (whether you're home or not), he won't need to head for the Golden Arches for sustenance.

Keep healthy snacks readily available.
Often kids will grab the first thing they see when they're hungry. Better for it to be a banana, apple, or granola bar than a Twinkie or a bag of Doritos. Try making the healthiest foods in your kitchen the most accessible. Stash the junk food away in little-used drawers or at the back of your cabinets. Keep the vegetables and fruits on prominent display.

Accommodate and encourage your teenager's healthy food preferences.

Take an any-port-in-a-storm approach to your teenager's meals. If you notice that your child has a taste for a particular fruit or vegetable, rejoice! Then take advantage of it. For example, let's say broccoli is one of the few vegetables your teen likes. Serve it as often as possible, in as many different forms as you can think of—in casseroles, as a side dish, smothered in cheese, on top of ice cream. . .well, you get the idea.

SECTION 12
RECOVERING FROM THE WORST

WHEN FOREVER ISN'T FOREVER ANYMORE

Marriage has been around for awhile, and for good reason: it was created by God way back in Genesis. Because of this, marriage is serious business. It's intended to be for life; it's a commitment between two people. Sure, it can be hard to stick to a commitment like this. But even though it can be tough, husbands and wives need to strive to keep a strong marriage—to communicate (speaking *and* listening), to look to the other's needs first, to reconcile their differences.

HELPING YOUR KIDS COPE AFTER A DIVORCE

Sometimes, sadly, these commitments are broken and a divorce is imminent. Helping your kids through the trauma of a divorce will be especially difficult because of the raw emotions that you are experiencing. Obviously, it's a task that will require quite a bit of strength on your part. In order to

DON'T FORGET

Where to Find Support

- Church
- Family
- Divorce recovery groups
- Friends
- Christian counseling

provide that strength, you need to make sure that you're receiving the help and support *you* need in order to deal with your own emotions as well as your child's.

Here are some tips to get you started as you and your children attempt to cope with life in the wake of a divorce.

Don't put your kids in the middle of the fight.

Regardless of who is at fault in the divorce or how you feel about your ex-spouse, don't drag your kids into the melee! Don't use custody as a way of getting revenge for past hurts inflicted by your spouse. Don't try to influence your kids' feelings toward your ex. Avoid situations in which your kids are forced to choose between you and your ex.

Your kids will know when they're being used as pawns. And their self-image will suffer as a result—along with their respect for and relationship with you *and* your ex-spouse.

Give your kids a chance to talk openly about their feelings.

Your kids will have plenty of questions about your divorce. You need to give them the chance (and the courage) to ask those questions. Keep in mind, though, that these question-and-answer sessions are no place for sugar-coated responses. If your kids are brave enough to ask direct questions, you need to be brave enough to give them straight answers.

Beyond answering their questions, you need to encourage your children to talk about their feelings regularly in the wake of the divorce. Be warned, though: The things they say may not always be pleasant. In fact, you should be prepared to bear some of the brunt of their resentment and anger about the situation. Resist the urge to get upset or to automatically defend yourself when your children share their feelings. Let them vent.

Don't underestimate the guilt your kids may be feeling.

More likely than not, your kids will blame themselves to some degree for the breakup of your marriage. Many kids of divorce believe that if they'd been a little better-behaved or a little more accommodating, their parents would still be together. Though their reasoning may seem irrational to us, it makes perfect sense to the kids.

That's why it's important for you to repeatedly and consistently remind your children that the fault for your divorce lies with you and your ex-spouse. If you can do so without bad-mouthing anyone, explain to your kids the chain of events that led to the breakup of your marriage. Help them see that they are completely blameless in the situation.

Provide as much stability as possible.

No one needs you more in the wake of a divorce than your children. Nothing is more important than spending time with them. With their world in an upheaval, they need to know that they can count on you to be there for them.

In the weeks and months following your divorce, scale back your social calendar so that you can spend every spare minute with your kids. Take them away for a vacation, if possible. Spend quality time with them. Let them know that though your marriage has ended, they still have a solid family base to depend on.

THE BRADY BUNCH NEVER LOOKED LIKE THIS

GETTING YOUR CHILD USED TO STEPSIBLINGS AND STEPPARENTS

Ever wonder how Mike and Carol Brady were able to combine their families so smoothly? They had scriptwriters. In the real world, you don't have that luxury. The best we can offer you are a couple of tips for making the transition easier for you and your child.

Remember the importance of time.

If you're remarrying, it means your child has either experienced the upheaval of divorce or the death of a parent. Either way, he's been dealt a serious blow, one that's difficult to recover from. Learning that he's going to be part of a blended family may bring back those feelings of upheaval all over again.

You see, what seems like stability to you may seem like uncharted and unsettling territory for your child. A new home, new rules, new house-mates, a new family—that's quite a bit for a child to digest. Give him time to come to grips with his new situation. It would be unfair for you to expect him to feel comfortable with the idea right away.

Obviously, the more understanding you and your new spouse offer concerning your child's feelings, the more likely it is that he will come to accept the arrangement—in time. The best thing you can do is remain patient and endure the occasional bumps (or, sometimes, the gaping potholes) in the road as you work to create a new family dynamic.

Be prepared to answer some difficult questions.

Chances are, your child is going to have some difficulty with the idea of a new parent. He's going to have some questions for you. Questions that may upset you. Questions like these:

- In the case of divorce: "Would you still be married to Dad/Mom if it weren't for him/her?"

- In the case of a spouse's death: "Do you love him/her as much as you loved Dad/Mom?"

- "Why do we need another person in our family?"

- "Do you love him/her as much as you love me?"

- "Do I have to call him/her 'Dad/Mom'?"

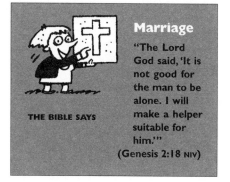

Marriage

THE BIBLE SAYS

"The Lord God said, 'It is not good for the man to be alone. I will make a helper suitable for him.'"
(Genesis 2:18 NIV)

Don't shy away from such questions or take offense at them. Instead, answer them with as much honesty and compassion as possible.

HEALING THE DEEPEST HURT

HELPING YOUR KIDS RECOVER FROM ABUSE

If you're consulting this section because you suspect (or know) that someone under your roof is abusing your children, put the book down right now and get your kids out of the house.

As a parent, your primary responsibility is to protect your children and keep them safe. If your home is not a safe haven, you must move your kids to someplace that is safe.

If you've already removed yourself and your children from the presence of the abuser, here are some steps you can take to help your children recover from the hurt that has been inflicted.

Seek professional help as a family.

The child abuse victim is not the only member of the family who suffers. Therefore, he's not the only one who needs help. If there

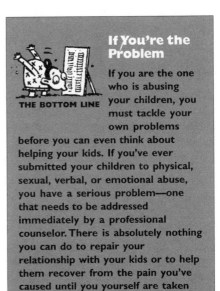

THE BOTTOM LINE

If You're the Problem

If you are the one who is abusing your children, you must tackle your own problems before you can even think about helping your kids. If you've ever submitted your children to physical, sexual, verbal, or emotional abuse, you have a serious problem—one that needs to be addressed immediately by a professional counselor. There is absolutely nothing you can do to repair your relationship with your kids or to help them recover from the pain you've caused until you yourself are taken care of.

are other children in the family who escaped the abuse, they will need to deal with the complicated emotions they may be experiencing. Likewise, depending on your role (unwitting or not) in the abusive situation, you likely have a jumble of feelings to sort out.

You may think your family is strong enough to work through the problem without any outside help. You're wrong. What's more, you're gambling with the lives of your children. You and your family need the help of trained professionals. At the very least, you need to know how to show sensitivity to and provide emotional support for the victim(s) of the abuse. Don't forget the powerful role the church and your pastors can play in counseling and supporting you. That's what they're there for: caring for members of the Body of Christ.

Work to regain the trust of your children.

In the aftermath of the abuse, you will have some tough questions to ask yourself. Where were you when the abuse was happening? Did you know anything about it? If so, what kept you from acting? Did you inadvertently enable the abuse? Most significantly, did you let your children down?

After you've answered those questions for yourself, you need to answer them for your children. You need to explain to them what prevented you from recognizing or stopping the abuse earlier. Admit any guilt you may be feeling. Seek forgiveness if you believe you let your kids down. Assure them that you will never make the same mistake again, that they can count on you to protect them from now on.

After you've worked through your emotions with a professional counselor, you need to sit down with your kids again and explain to them what you've learned about yourself and how your newfound knowledge will affect their future.

Help your children understand the importance of breaking the cycle of abuse.

What's true of history is true of child abuse. Those who don't learn from it are doomed to repeat it. Statistics indicate that the overwhelming majority of child abusers were themselves victims of abuse. Do not allow your children to become part of this disturbing trend.

Using whatever resources are available to you, help your children understand the differences between normal relationship patterns and dysfunctional ones. Help them understand the differences between healthy and unhealthy anger management. More than anything else, though, help them understand their worth as individuals.

THE LONG GOOD-BYE

RECOVERING FROM THE DEATH OF A FRIEND OR FAMILY MEMBER

Christians live with the assurance that death is not the end, that a better place awaits us when this life is over. Revelation 21:4 tells us, "[Jesus] will wipe every tear from their eyes. There will be no more death or mourning or crying or pain, for the old order of things has passed away." Even with that assurance, though, we cannot help but be overwhelmed by grief and loneliness when a loved one dies.

As a parent, you have a responsibility to care not only for your own emotional well-being in the face of such a tragedy, but also for your children's well-being. Here are a few suggestions you might want to consider.

Recognize that the expression of grief is unique from person to person.

Different people experience grief in different ways. There is no one pattern that "healthy" people follow when they lose a loved one. It would be a mistake for you to try to persuade your kids to adhere to a particular pattern of expressions. For example, when you feel like crying, your child may feel like laughing. When you feel lonely, he may feel angry. All of these are normal reactions.

The best thing you can do for your children is to be there for them through all of their stages of grief, however "inappropriate" some of those stages may seem at the time. A listening ear and an empathetic spirit are two of the best gifts anyone could hope to receive after losing a loved one.

Keep the person's memory alive.

You may find it difficult to talk about a loved one after he's gone. That's a normal reaction to death. Usually the difficulty is due to the fear of stirring up emotions. People are afraid that mentioning the loved one's name will break open an emotional dam, causing a fresh flood of tears.

Actually, that's a very real possibility—at first. As time goes by, though, you'll find that the tears are replaced by a less-pronounced sense of sadness and loss, and then by a warm nostalgia.

Regardless of the emotions that may result, you need to keep your loved one's memory alive— for your sake and for the sake of your children. Don't be afraid of your feelings and memories. Embrace them! Learn to laugh and cry with your children as you recall the things that made your loved one so special.

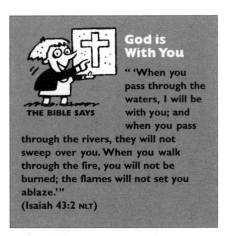

God is With You

THE BIBLE SAYS " 'When you pass through the waters, I will be with you; and when you pass through the rivers, they will not sweep over you. When you walk through the fire, you will not be burned; the flames will not set you ablaze.' "
(Isaiah 43:2 NLT)

Recognize that some days will be more difficult than others.

Keep in mind that special days bring back special memories—memories that often produce a fresh wave of sadness and grief. Holidays, birthdays, and anniversaries are most likely to trigger emotions in your kids. Mark these days on your calendar to remind yourself to do something special to celebrate, relive, and help your kids get through these times.

Of course, your kids are likely to have special days of their own etched in their minds. For example, memories of a now-deceased loved one in the stands during a high school football game may cause some melancholy feelings when the next football season rolls around. Likewise, memories of past family vacations may cause some sadness when summer vacation rolls around.

Observe these special days by engaging your kids in conversation about their thoughts and feelings. Encourage them to share both their memories and their feelings of sadness and loss.

CLEAR AND PRESENT DANGER

FINDING HELP FOR YOUR KID'S DEPRESSION, EATING DISORDERS, OR SUBSTANCE ABUSE

Most of the problems kids face are relatively minor and easily resolved. However, there are a few adolescent struggles that require careful attention. If you suspect that your child is battling a serious problem, it's up to you to do something about it.

Don't delay.

If your child is battling severe depression, an eating disorder (such as anorexia or bulimia), or alcohol or drug abuse, you've got a medical

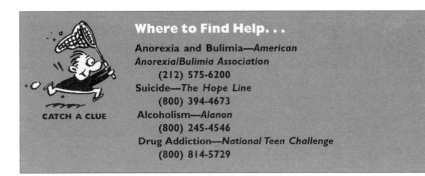

CATCH A CLUE

Where to Find Help. . .

Anorexia and Bulimia—*American Anorexia/Bulimia Association*
    (212) 575-6200
Suicide—*The Hope Line*
    (800) 394-4673
Alcoholism—*Alanon*
    (800) 245-4546
    Drug Addiction—*National Teen Challenge*
    (800) 814-5729

emergency on your hands. Treat it that way. We're not suggesting that you call 911 if you find marijuana in your kid's room. However, we *are* suggesting that the longer you delay in addressing the problem, the more jeopardy you're putting your child in. Worst-case scenarios in all three of the situations we just described involve the death of your child. That fact alone should propel you into immediate action.

Turn to the right people for assistance.

Depending on the severity and duration of your child's problem, your first call should be either to your doctor or your pastor. If it's a medical emergency, call your primary health-care provider. If your child is not in immediate danger, call your pastor. Both of these professionals will protect your child's privacy. Both should also be able to give you the names of people and organizations specifically trained to help your child through his/her problems.

If you have friends you can confide in, do so. You may be surprised to learn that they or someone they know went through a similar experience. Consult the library or even the phone book for the names of clinics or counselors in your area who can help you. After you've compiled a list of names, conduct phone or office interviews to find the one you think will work best for your child.

Be supportive, but firm.

The road to recovery is long and rocky. Many times along the way you and your child will get tired, frustrated, and disappointed. It's important that you keep your focus and composure during these discouraging times. You don't know how much your "togetherness" means to your child. Don't let her down—and don't allow her to let herself down.

When your child's spirit, resolve, or strength starts to flag, inject a fresh supply of support and encouragement. Do not allow failure to become an option during the recovery or rehabilitation process.

You cannot fight the battle for your child, but you can fight it with her. And with the Lord as the third member of your triumvirate, there's nothing your child can't overcome. Keep in mind the words of Ecclesiastes 4:9–12: "Two are better than one, because they have a good return for their work: If one falls down, his friend can help him up. But pity the man who falls and has no one to help him up! Also, if two lie down together, they will keep warm. But how can one keep warm alone? Though one may be overpowered, two can defend themselves. A cord of three strands is not quickly broken."

THE LITTLEST CARETAKERS

DEALING WITH AN ILLNESS IN THE FAMILY

A serious illness will test your family's mettle, but it doesn't have to destroy its spirit. Here are some steps you can take to help your kids cope with the serious medical condition of a close family member.

Don't underestimate your kids' ability to cope.

Children are more resilient than you might imagine. They tend to fret more about the unknown than the known. So if you're keeping news of an illness from your kids in an effort to shield them from the truth, you might be doing more harm than good. Kids aren't stupid. They know when

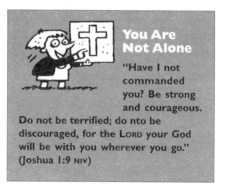

You Are Not Alone

"Have I not commanded you? Be strong and courageous. Do not be terrified; do nto be discouraged, for the LORD your God will be with you wherever you go." (Joshua 1:9 NIV)

something's up. Not knowing the details of what's going on will usually only compound their unsettled feelings. Give your kids a chance to surprise you with their strength. Give them the truth.

Talk openly and responsibly about the illness.

Once you've broached the subject of the illness, be prepared to answer your kids' questions about it. Sure, some of their queries may be tough to face. Some may not be phrased as tactfully as you might like. But you can be sure that the questions are from their heart—and that alone makes them deserving of an answer.

While it's important to talk openly, it's also important that you never talk flippantly about the illness. Morbid humor may be a useful coping mechanism for some people, but it's probably not the approach you should take with your kids. Instead, be prepared with honest answers expressed in a sensitive manner.

Give your kids some caretaking responsibilities.

Don't consign your kids to the role of mere spectators of the illness. Enroll them in the fight. Give them household responsibilities that will lighten the load for you (and/or the person suffering from the illness). Give your young ones the opportunity to feel like they're contributing to the family's well-being, whether it's through cleaning the house, making meals, or doing the grocery shopping. You'll find that your entire family benefits as a result.

INDEX

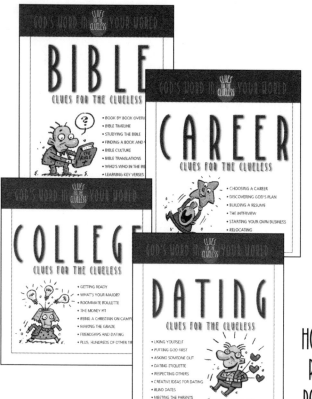